KT-226-685

THINGS YOU DIDN'T KNOW, YOU DIDN'T KNOW!

GRAEME DONALD

London
UNWIN PAPERBACKS

Boston   Sydney

First published by Unwin Paperbacks 1985
Reprinted 1985 (twice)

UNWIN® PAPERBACKS
40 Museum Street, London WC1A 1LU, UK

Unwin Paperbacks
Park Lane, Hemel Hempstead, Herts HP2 4TE, UK

Allen & Unwin (Australia) Ltd
8 Napier Street, North Sydney, NSW 2060, Australia

Unwin Paperbacks with the
Port Nicholson Press
PO Box 11–838 Wellington, New Zealand

© Jocelyn Films Ltd, 1985

British Library Cataloguing in Publication Data

Donald, Graeme
  Things you didn't know you didn't know.
  1. Curiosities and wonders
  I. Title
032'.02   AG243
ISBN 0-04-827146-2

Set in 10 on 11½ point Sabon by Columns, Reading, Berkshire
and printed in Great Britain by
Cox & Wyman Ltd, Reading, Berkshire

For Di

Contents

ARMED FORCES

THE ANDREW

This still common nickname for the Royal Navy was born back in the days of the Napoleonic Wars when the waterfronts and docklands of England were teeming with press gangs indulging in their now well-known gentle form of recruitment. The senior press officer of Portsmouth was then one Andrew Miller, a gentleman unequalled in zeal and success. He introduced so many young men to a life on the ocean waves that his name became synonymous with the Navy itself. Even the warships themselves became generally known as 'Andrew Millers'.

Actually, the legislation raised to support the activities of the press gangs has never been repealed, although an act of 1835 states that any man who wakes up at sea with a sore head must be released after five years' service.

BAG OR BAGGAGE

When the Army of yesteryear went on the move, it was rarely the logistically planned and organised affair that it is today. Not only was the available transport less efficient but there were countless numbers of hangers-on and camp followers. A large proportion of these tended to be women who would earn a living by providing laundry and cleaning services, or by providing other services that indicated their total misunderstanding of the old maxim, 'An army marches on its stomach'. *Hors de Combat*, you might say. All such persons travelled at the rear of the column with the pack-mules carrying the baggage and personal effects of the officers, and it was not long before the term 'bag' moved into general usage as an unkind description of a woman to whom nature had been less than generous.

Because of the sticky fingers of most of the people who accompanied the baggage train, officers always instructed their aides to travel with and guard the mules transporting their possessions. The packsaddles were called 'bats' – hence 'batman'.

BALACLAVA AND CARDIGAN
During the Crimean War, there was a national drive to get all the women of England knitting at a great rate of knots to produce easy-to-make but practical woollen garments to protect the British troops from the Russian winter. Since some of the bloodiest fighting took place at Balaclava, the knitted helmets were thus named, and the accompanying jackets named after Lord Cardigan, famous for leading the Light Brigade into history.

BERSERK
Properly, this is the name of the war-hero of Scandinavian mythology who was famed for entering battle clad only in bearskin. His name is based on one of two possibilities, *ber sark* or *boer serce*, both of which are Norse and mean 'bear-shirt' and 'bare of mail' respectively. Early Britons first encountered the old Norse tactic of 'going berserk' or 'berserking' back in the days when the Vikings used to pop across to places like Whitby and Scarborough for some rape and pillage. When attacking, they would emulate their hero by charging the enemy howling and gnashing at their shields the while – a somewhat undignified procedure which, although bad for the bridgework, was highly effective in scaring the goatskins of the locals who rapidly adopted the expression to describe anyone acting in a wild and uncontrollable manner.

The Vikings believed that the berserk rage was granted to a warrior from Odin himself, and that once the rage passed from him he was left totally weak and defenceless.

4

BIG BERTHA

A fairly popular sobriquet for a woman possessed of a less than sylphlike figure which started out in life as a nickname applied by the press to the massive artillery piece used by the Germans in 1918 to shell Paris from a distance of 76 miles. An enormous, cumbersome thing weighing 142 tons and firing a 264lb shell, it was anything but practical in that the barrel needed changing after eleven rounds, and was dubbed Big Bertha because it had been made in the armament factories belonging to Frau Bertha Krupp.

BIKINI

This very pleasant garment to see a pretty girl in, or half out of, as is more often the case today, has its etymological roots in something far more sinister than scanty-pantied maidens frolicking on sun-kissed beaches, for it is named after Bikini Atoll which, prior to the Second World War, was known as Escholtz Atoll in the Marshall Islands. In 1946, Bikini was chosen by the United States as an atomic test site so, despite the protestations of the small population that they were quite unworthy of the honour, they were all evicted and moved to an island about 130 miles away so that their betters could spend the next twelve years or so popping off atomic devices to see what would happen to the place.

In the same year as the first test, a French car engineer named Louis Reard joined his mother's clothing company and, in response to a call for something new and revolutionary, came up with the first two-piece swimsuit. He said that he named it the 'bikini' due to the similar effect of a beautiful woman so clad and the atomic bomb dropped on the island – a joke that the wildlife and marine life on and around Bikini would not have appreciated.

BRASS MONKEY WEATHER

Hardly the kind of observation on prevailing inclement weather calculated to get you invited back to the next garden party at the vicarage, but the only connection with simian reproductive equipment would be in the minds of those offended.

The word 'monkey' used to be widespread in the gunnery slang of the days of the old muzzle-loading pieces. Not only could it be applied to any gun or cannon, but also to its operators – e.g. 'powder monkey'. The suffix 'monkey' moved into general usage and was tagged on to many trades; mechanics in the States still get called 'grease monkeys'. Anyway, the monkey in question here was a heavy brass square located on the deck beside a ship's cannon, its purpose being to hold a small stack of ammunition. Since it was of great use to a gun crew, it received the affectionate name, 'brass monkey', as if it were another member of the team. It is, if you like, a term similar to 'dumb waiter'.

Naval humour being what it always has been, it would be naïve in the extreme not to suppose that the crude interpretation was not in mind when the expression was 'punned' and it is doubtful that we will ever hear it from the lips of a BBC weatherman.

CHAUVINISM

The relatively obscure term 'chauvinism' with its pure meaning of a blind, irrational adherence to any cause, has been with us since the mid–late 1800s, but it took the Women's Liberation Movement of the sixties to save it from redundancy by sweeping it into the public ken with their battle cry of 'male chauvinist pig'. Since the kind of male to whom this tag really applies is tedious in the extreme, one cannot help wondering why the more cutting 'male chauvinist boar' was not coined. Even more ironic is the fact that the women chose a word that had been built squarely on the shoulders of a man's name; one Nicolas Chauvin, to be precise.

Chauvin was a wounded veteran of the Napoleonic campaigns and was so wildly fanatical in his admiration for his hero that he became something of a laughing stock around Paris. Even after Boney was safely tucked up on St Helena and France was desperately trying to forget all about him and get back to some semblance of normality, Chauvin was still there playing the same old song. Such a spectacle did he make of himself that playwrights such as Scribe and Cogniard caricatured him in farces.

CLOSE-QUARTERS

Actually, the first word in the heading is 'close' as in shut, not as in near. Originally called 'close-fights', these were like little wooden blockhouses built on the decks of merchantmen. In the event of a boarding seeming imminent, certain members of the crew could install themselves with musket and shot to create a withering crossfire on the decks. Privateers who boarded, expecting to engage in hand-to-hand combat, found themselves totally alone and possessed of a sudden, irrational desire to jump over the side. There are numerous well-documented cases of seemingly harmless merchantmen inflicting wholesale slaughter on the crews of fully armed men-of-war who made the mistake of boarding with intent to take the ship as prize.

Naturally enough, when civvy street picked up the expression, it was in the form of 'close' as in near, for when the close-fights came into play, the enemy were, by necessity, very close indeed.

CRAVAT

In the 1600s, Croatian mercenaries, called 'Khruvats' in their native Slavonic tongue, served as border guards along the Turkish borders of the Hapsburg territories, some later drifting to serve the French crown. When Louis XIV decided to form a new regiment, he called it the Royal Cravat – the closest that the French tongue could get to 'Khruvat'. The most striking part of the new regiment's uniform which the Croatian influence had given rise to, was a loosely tied neck-scarf. Since men's fashion has always mimicked the military, it was not long before French civilians were sporting similar items.

CUT TO THE QUICK

This phrase and the expression 'the quick and the dead' are about the only examples left where the word 'quick' appears in its true meaning. The word really means 'alive' or 'living' and the above used to be a battlefield expression to denote a sword-blow severe enough to penetrate armour and bite into the body beneath it, into the living flesh, in other words. It was the emergence of expressions like 'look lively' or 'look alive' that began overlaying the word 'quick' with connotations of speed.

DEADLINE

This term, that now means nothing more sinister than the fixed and unchangeable date for the completion of a specific task, was born in one of the most disgraceful POW camps of the American Civil War – Andersonville. In this hell-hole, whose commanding officer, Captain Henry Wirz, was hanged after the war, over 30,000 Union soldiers were held in the one stockade in atrocious conditions, and only about half of them walked out. Wirz it was who came up with the simple idea of a 'deadline' to discourage escape. Some distance in from the stockade walls was a line drawn around the whole camp, and any prisoner seen crossing the line was automatically assumed to be attempting to escape and was shot out of hand. The device and the term was rapidly adopted by numerous other camps, but it was the war crimes of Wirz that gave the term to the public.

DERRICK (AS IN HOIST)

In the late 1500s, a small fleet under the command of the Earl of Essex, mounted an attack upon the Spanish mainland and sacked Cadiz. Whilst ashore both officers and men picked up everything of value that was not nailed down and scurried back to their ships with booty a-plenty for the English crown. In all the excitement, some of the chaps forgot about a few little baubles secreted about their persons, a lapse of memory considered treasonable by Essex who had gone to Cadiz to rip off the Spaniards in the name of queen and country, not private enterprise. Being a liberal-minded sort of fellow, he decided that all of them should be strung up from the yard-arms; a sentence none too popular with the fleet, who thought the activities of Mr Derrick and his pals to be fair game, and there was a conspicuous lack of volunteers to carry out the hanging.

With black humour, Derrick himself stepped into the breech and set about decorating the spars of Essex's flagship with his own companions, in recognition of which his own sentence was commuted to a flogging round the fleet, which in itself could amount to a death sentence, but Derrick survived. Tales of this charade spread across England and Derrick became something of a celebrity who capitalised on his new-found skills with the anodyne necklace by taking up the position of hangman at Tyburn. His name soon became synonymous with the gibbet and, due to his previous exploits, the nickname spread to the hoisting device on ships.

As an interesting side-note to history, the wheel turned full circle for Essex and Derrick for, when the former was sentenced to death for conspiracy against the crown in 1601, it was the latter whose job it was to deprive him of this mortal coil.

FACE THE MUSIC

In most Western armies, any officer being cashiered from his regiment is required to stand on the parade ground and face the drum squad who tap slowly while the reasons for the man's dismissal are read out and his uniform defaced and stripped of insignia.

FAGGING

This particularly unhealthy peculiarity of the British public school system is named after a dodge once common to both the Army and the Navy, whereby one man would stand in for another on muster to cover the fact that the latter was AWOL. Since the usual roll call consisted of names being called out to be answered by a shout of 'Aye', the ruse was invariably successful. In the Army, fagging even went so far as one man undertaking to do another's full tour of duty when a new regiment was being raised. The abbreviated form of 'fag' was later applied to young schoolboys forced to undertake tasks by older ones.

The reason why the term 'faggot' was chosen in the first place is a trifle obscure, but it could well be in allusion to the bundles of twigs and small sticks bound together into faggots to serve as a substitute fuel for the logs that the poor could not afford or obtain. As a final development born of the widespread and not totally unfounded suspicion that public schools are a breeding ground, if that be the right term, for homosexuals, 'fag' and 'faggot' took on such meaning, thus insinuating a more intimate relationship than was proper between the senior boy and his fag.

FIFTH COLUMN
It was General Emile Mola who coined this phrase in 1936 during the Spanish Civil War, and it remains with us today to describe traitors or infiltrators working within a country they aim to destroy. When talking on the radio, just prior to his forces advancing in four columns to encircle Madrid, Mola was asked if he thought such a force to be up to the task of taking the city. In his answer he said that it was because he had a 'fifth column' already inside the city waiting to strike, meaning, of course, preplanted spies and saboteurs. Although it was Mola who coined the expression, it was Hemingway who popularised it with his play of the same title.

FLAK
This word, now used for harassment or severe criticism, is a hand-me-down from the Second World War and derives, oddly enough, from the German *fliegerabwehr-kanone*, which meant anti-aircraft fire. No wonder we shortened it!

FLASH IN THE PAN
Basically this means a great deal of show but little effective action, or an initial burst of enthusiasm followed by nothing at all. In the early days of flintlock weapons, which were notoriously unreliable, it was far from uncommon for the flint to spark and ignite the priming charge in the pan below, but for this 'flash in the pan' to fail to ignite the main charge in the barrel.

FORLORN HOPE

Despite it seeming completely logical and very obvious, the second word in the heading has nothing to do with the term 'hope' in the sense of aspiration. Similar in meaning to the French *enfants perdus*, *verloren hoop* was a Dutch military expression to describe the first wave of men sent in to test out the enemy strength. It means 'lost troop.' Due to a misunderstanding in civvy street, or to deliberate alteration by folk etymology, 'forlorn hope' soon became the accepted form which, considering that there was faint hope of survival for such men, is fair enough at the end of the day.

FREELANCE

Coined as recently as 1820 by Sir Walter Scott, this term for an independent operator alludes to medieval mercenaries whose lances were free from any allegiance. The word 'lance' is best known in military circles by its use in the rank of 'lance corporal' which is ultimately based on the old Italian designation of *lancia spezzata* – broken lance – as applied to an experienced soldier who had 'broken his lance', or bloodied himself, on active service. The sleeve chevron insignia of NCOs is meant to be reminiscent of a lance snapped in two.

FULL TILT

When the knights of old intended to engage an enemy, the lance was gradually lowered from the vertical to the horizontal as the two opponents closed. As can be imagined, holding a long lance at right angles to the body as a horse bumps away across uneven ground, is going to put quite a strain on a knight who, in the interests of conserving his energy for the serious business of skewering his fellow man, did not fully lower (or 'tilt' as the action was termed) his lance until he had reached top speed and was almost in range of his objective. So, when the lance was at full tilt, the knight was travelling at top speed.

GENOCIDE

Oddly enough, it was not until 1948 that genocide became a crime under International Law as a result of a motion passed by the United Nations General Assembly, which raised a rather difficult point in 1945 when the Allies wanted to try Nazi war criminals. Genocide, as a word, was the brainchild of one Professor Raphael Lemkin of Duke University, Durham, North Carolina and had been 'invented' for the indictment at Nuremburg. Lemkin built on the Greek *genos* and the Latin *caedere* – meaning 'race' and 'to kill' respectively.

As stated, the employment of this totally new charge produced a legal dilemma that caused several judges invited to sit to decline. Since there was no legislation under the current International Law concerning genocide, no one could be tried for it.

GERONIMO – AS A WAR CRY

In this country, this long dead warrior's name is only really used in a tongue-in-cheek manner, a bit like a Tarzan call before mock heroics. The sarcasm implied by its use is most likely there because we picked up the shout from the Americans when they were considered to be 'over paid, over-sexed and over here'.

The whole thing began back in the formative days of the United States 82nd Airborne Division which had its paratroop training camps at Lafayette in Indiana. In the summer of 1938, the new batch of recruits were given leave on the day before their first full-drill jump from a real plane. Most drifted into the town and a fair number went to the local cinema which was showing a new film entitled 'Geronimo'. The film included a stunt that was based on a real incident in the Indian's life, when he rode off a near vertical cliff, named Medicine Bluffs, in Oklahoma, to escape his Army pursuers who, quite sensibly, decided not to follow suit. In the film, the stuntman yelled, 'Geronimo!' as he plummeted into the river, an incident that caused much sniggering and nervous shifting about in seats amongst each successive audience who knew only too well that they themselves had a date with gravity next morning.

Up into the wide blue yonder they duly flew the next day and, before hurling themselves bodily into same with nothing 'twixt them and extinction but a fine silk mushroom, many mimicked the stuntman in what was most likely a nervous attempt to cover up their fears that the parachute packers might have had one too many themselves the night before. And that was that! The next thing that anyone knew, all the recruits were yelling, 'Geronimo!' and the 82nd had little choice but to adopt it formally as a battle-cry.

GLASSHOUSE – IN THE

This military equivalent of 'clink' or 'stir' is quickly explained in that the famous North Camp of Aldershot's military prison had a glass roof at one time.

GONE FOR A BURTON

Offhand, and with the exception of the following entry, it is difficult to think of any other contribution to current English made by the RAF, whose only excuse can be that it is the newest of the three services and has not been around long enough to have had much effect on its native tongue.

As a stiff upper-lipism for having been shot down,

especially over the sea, this expression was born in Second World War RAF mess parlance as the result of a highly successful advertising campaign by Burton Ales. Everywhere there were posters depicting groups of people, an orchestra, troops on parade, etc. with one person very obviously missing. The never-changing caption was 'Gone for a Burton!' Its RAF use was reinforced by the fact that the sea had long been known as 'The Drink'.

GREMLIN

Recently made film stars by a peculiar film of the same name, these less than winsome creatures of paranoid imagination are generally held responsible for all the inexplicable hostility of inanimate objects, and were named by a squadron of Bomber Command who were unlucky enough to be granted the remoteness of India's North-West Frontier for a base. The tranquility of their rugged mountain fastness was lost on the Brylcreem boys posted there, they being unimpressed with the total lack of nightlife, general facilities, supplies, the irregularity of mail, and so forth. The hot, dry, dusty atmosphere played hell with the aero-engines, carburettor and air filtration problems being the most common causes of being grounded. The pilots invented, named and blamed the Gremlins. They made the name up from *Grimm's Fairy Tales* and 'Fremlin' – the former being the only book in the station's library and the latter being the name of a brand of beer which was the only drink available in the mess bar.

GRENADE

Fruit seems to loom large in the life of these unpleasant yet highly effective devices. Popularly known as 'pineapples', we based our term on the French nickname, *pomme granate* – meaning pomegranate, or, quite literally 'seedy apple', in allusion to the shrapnel thrown by such devices.

HARBINGER

It is doubtless because of the original application of this word that it is almost invariably employed to describe some portent or person regarded as the bringer of ill news. Derived from the Old German words *heri* and *berga* which mean 'army' and 'shelter' respectively, this used to be the title of an officer responsible for preceding an army to establish adequate lodgings. So, when a harbinger turned up in a village or town it usually boded ill for the locals who knew that they were going to have soldiers billeted on them, and that they would probably have to feed and house them for a short time for no return. The only people who were ever happy to see a harbinger were the innkeepers and the local 'anthology of pros'.

HAVOC

Another term of military origin that has lost its murderous connotations on its passage through time. The cry of 'Havoc!' before a battle meant that the army was to attack without mercy and kill everyone that they could.

HOIST BY ONE'S OWN PETARD

In medieval warfare, a petard was a kind of mine used to blow a breach in castle walls or to remove the gates. Soldiers did not tend to fall over each other in their anxiety to volunteer for the job of carrying these devices to the target, for not only did those of an unsporting disposition within the castle consider it fair game to take repeated pot shots at the unfortunate sapper and pour boiling oil on him as he tried to position his charge, but the bombs themselves were notoriously unreliable, quite often capriciously detonating as soon as the match came anywhere near them. In short, the man placing the petard was as likely to get blown up (hoist) as get clear.

It must be assumed that the noise they made on detonation was strange, to say the least, for, ultimately based on the French verb *peter* — meaning 'to fart', *petarde* originally meant 'a succession of farts as released by a horse'. This somewhat crude derivation makes 'petard' an etymological bedfellow of the part-ridge of pear tree fame. The Greeks named the bird *perdix* — the farter — due to the pronounced whirring noise the creature makes with its wings during take-off.

HOOKER

This word for prostitute has nothing to do with the idea of women 'hooking' their clients. The term arose in America, in Manhattan, to be precise, where, in the nineteenth century, the term was applied to the girls who worked the infamous waterfronts of Corlear's Hook. Until the outbreak of the Civil War 'hooker' was strictly a term local to the New York area; it took the earthy proclivities of one of the Union's more boisterous generals to give the word to a no doubt grateful nation.

General Joseph Hooker was once described by Charles Francis Adams, Minister to Great Britain and son of the sixth President, as 'a man of blemished character whose headquarters was a place that no self-respecting man liked to go and no decent woman could go, for it can only be described as a combination of bar-room and brothel'. On the other hand, Hooker was uncommonly well liked by his own men, and soldiers from other regiments demonstrated their touching affection for the man by constantly submitting transfer requests. Reading between the lines, he must also have been something of a tactical genius, for, the annoyance of the war itself permitting, other high-ranking officers never missed the chance to seek out his camp and spend the night there, no doubt seeking his advice on matters military.

With the massive concentration of troops in and around Washington at the time, it was a natural development that the city's red light district would grow to ensure that supply met demand. Almost overnight, the area became known as 'Hooker's Division' and, with the constant movement of troops in and out of the city, the term spread like wildfire.

JEEP

When the American Army decided that it wanted a tough little all-terrains vehicle, motor-factories vied with each other to submit designs and quotations. Eventually, decisions were made, contracts were awarded and production instigated, but we have to thank GI Joe for its present name. Sublimely ignorant of all the wheeling and dealing that had gone on to grab a piece of the best action to come out of an Army contract for some time, he had his nose buried safely in a comic.

In 1937, some three years before the events mentioned above, E.C. Segar had introduced a new character to his ever-popular 'Popeye' cartoon strip. 'Eugene the Jeep', as this new edition was known to his numerous fans, was a tough little dog-like creature who was virtually indestructible and could become invisible at will. Since the GIs thought the characteristics of the new issue vehicles to be so similar to the cartoon animal, except that one ran on orchids and the other on petrol, the title of 'jeep' was promptly bestowed.

JERRY CAN

This container's tale is short and to the point. The British Army stole the design from those cans that were standard issue to the German Afrika Korps.

JINGOISM

Originally a piece of sixteenth-century magician's gibberish, 'jingo' used to stand as a substitute for 'God', as did 'gosh' and 'golly'. Its transfer to the application currently understood, namely, the British brand of excessive nationalism and sabre-rattling, occurred via the offices of a music hall song written by a chap called G.W.Hunt, in 1877, and first sung by The Great MacDermott.

Around that time, there was a tremendous amount of anti-Russian feeling; the Crimean War was not long over and now the Bear was preparing to make a meal of Turkey, to whose aid Britain was preparing to go. The song, which included the lines: 'We don't want to fight, but by Jingo if we do, / We've got the ships, we've got the men, and we've got the money too', went down great guns with the armchair generals who were all in favour of some sport with the Russians, providing that it was someone other than them who had to go out and risk the removal of various appendages by a bunch of blood-crazed Cossacks. It became a kind of battle hymn for the same type of people pandered to by the popular press during the recent Argentinian affair, when a 'newspaper' exhibited a 'Kill an Argie and win a Metro' mentality.

LACONIC

The ancient Spartans were noted for many things, but never for being prone to verbosity. Their tight-lippedness was so famous that the name of their land, Laconia, formed the foundation of the above term. One of the nicest examples, no doubt apocryphal, of their brevity of speech, relates to the time when Philip of Macedonia, with whom they were constantly at loggerheads, wrote to the Spartan Council threatening war. His message ended with the boast, 'If I enter Laconia, I will level Lacedaemonia (the capital city) to the ground.' The reply that he supposedly received was, 'If'.

LOCK, STOCK AND BARREL

This is an old Armyism still widely used to mean the whole kit and caboodle. It dates from the days of the old flintlock weapons which comprised three basic components, the lock, or firing mechanism, the stock and the barrel.

MARTINET

As a term for any rabid disciplinarian, this word is taken, quite unfairly, from the name of Jean Martinet, Commander-in-Chief of the King's Own Infantry Regiment in the reign of Louis XIV. The biggest drawback of Martinet's command was that he was constantly saddled with a succession of spoilt aristocratic brats whose fathers had bought them a regiment to play with; the only requirement, apart from money and background, being that they served as a platoon commander under Martinet. His job it was to instil some professionalism into these idiots to reduce marginally the wholesale butchery that tended to occur when large numbers of men were placed under the command of some mentally deficient 'sonovtherich', whose idea of military proficiency was restricted to posing round Paris in a specially tailored uniform.

Many of these dashing young blades left smarting from their stay with Martinet. They took with them a grudge and such a host of grossly exaggerated or totally untrue stories, painting Martinet as some kind of eccentric, that his false reputation spread throughout the entire Army. There is a myth that he was killed at the siege of Duisberg, shot in the back by his own men, whereas in truth he was killed by a stray salvo from his own artillery. The fact that a Swiss officer near to him at the time, was named Soury, gave rise to the well-known military pun that Duisberg only cost the King a martin and a mouse.

MOLOTOV COCKTAIL

Despite the use of Molotov's name, it was not the Russians who first used or named these primitive yet highly effective anti-tank devices. It was the underarmed Finns who developed them to use against their Russian invaders of 1939–40 and, since Molotov was the then Russian Minister of Foreign Affairs, the Finns thought it fitting to use his name.

MORRIS DANCING

Difficult as it may be to imagine a load of soldiers cavorting about with bells on their toes and bonking each other on the head with balloons, this most bizarre of all British folk traditions has its roots firmly in military dancing. It was introduced to England a little over 500 years ago by, it is believed, John O'Gaunt when he returned from Spain where his own soldiers had contracted the disease from the Moorish conscripts in the Spanish Army, whose weird style of war-dancing formed the basis of current Morris tradition. The very word 'Morris' is a corruption of 'Moorish' and in earlier times the dancers would always 'black up' before performing. Actually the Moors' style was not as unique as it seems at first glance. The Greeks were only on the other side of the Mediterranean, and there is nothing guaranteed to look more like a bunch of big tinkerbells than a group of Greek soldiers in traditional dress uniforms going through one of their routines.

NAIL YOUR COLOURS TO THE MAST

Needless to say, the colours in question are the ones flying from the masthead of a ship of the line of yesteryear. In battle, capitulation could be indicated to the enemy by striking, or lowering, your colours, something which you could not do if some lunatic had nailed them to the mast ensuring that the ship had to see the battle through to the end, either victorious or sunk.

Flags have given rise to several other expressions, such as 'with flying colours', which does, of course, mean victorious. Also, when a ship crossed the path of another belonging to a senior commander, it was considered common courtesy to lower the colours a bit in a gesture of respect. The height that the colours flew at was determined by a series of pegs at the base of the mast – hence 'to take someone down a peg or two'.

NOT ENOUGH ROOM TO SWING A CAT

Not that the idea is without its cruelly amusing side, but the notion that the four-legged variety of cat is involved here is totally erroneous. Of naval origin, this refers not to the ship's mouser but to the infamous cat o' nine tails, which was incapable of being swung round in the cramped sleeping quarters endured by the sailors. It was because of these very conditions and low ceilings that the Navy, to this day, enjoys the privilege of being allowed to toast the Queen whilst remaining seated.

PLONK

This is probably the most common remainder of a host of words based on a kind of dog-Franglais which entered English during the trench fighting in northern France in the First World War. 'Plonk' is a bastardised form of *blanc* as in *vin blanc*; other examples being 'napoo' meaning 'nothing' and built on *Il n'y en a plus* and 'toodeloo' which is the tortured offspring of '*à tout à l'heure*' – the French for 'see you soon'.

PIPE DOWN

In naval parlance, this was the special tune played on the boatswain's pipe last thing at night. This signal called for all hands to turn in, all lights to be extinguished and silence on the mess decks.

PITCHED BATTLE

Although it is tempting to assume that this derives from Millwall Football Club, it is in fact of much older origin. Communications being what they were in the old days, it was quite common for minor wars to be over and done with before half the country even heard about them. Great armies would set out to find each other and spend days staggering round the countryside looking for someone to lay into. Because of this, really important dust-ups tended to be prearranged affairs that were always 'pitched', meaning that they were held at mutually agreed sites.

PYRRHIC VICTORY

The name given to a victory gained at such crippling losses that it is virtually impossible to tell the victors from the vanquished. This comes from the name of Pyrrhus, king of Epirus, who defeated Valerius Laevinus and his Roman forces at the battle of Heraclea in 281 BC. After surveying the scene of his triumph, the victor is recorded as saying: 'One more such victory and we are lost.' The battle in question is sometimes erroneously cited as being Asculum, which Pyrrhus won in 279 BC.

QUARTER – TO GRANT

In days of old when knights were etc., chivalry was in all probability as rare a commodity as it is today, which is presumably why the nobility reserved it for those who could best appreciate it – themselves! In such times, a knight was the most sophisticated piece of war machinery available and, if he was captured in battle, his own side would pay to get him back; nobody bothered about taking cannon-fodder for ransom because they were not worth the food to keep them alive. While the price and details were being sorted out, the knight was accommodated, or granted living quarters, the cost of which was loaded on to the ransom.

QUISLING

Although in pure terms this should be applied to a collaborating traitor, this is increasingly heard in the sense of 'sneak' or 'snitch'. The original was Vidkun Quisling who was the puppet leader of the Norwegian State Council appointed by the Nazis during the occupation. His fellow countrymen showed their appreciation for his guidance through such troubled times by putting him up against a wall and shooting him at the first available opportunity.

ROUND ROBIN

Petitions of grievance were troublesome things for the monarchs of old, for they tended to interrupt the day's pleasures. In an effort to dissuade the great unwashed from cluttering up their palaces snivelling about starvation and other privations that were their just desserts, it was standard practice to hold the threat of death over the first signatory should the petition be considered unwarranted. This tended to make it difficult to get a petition off the ground. Undeterred, the downtrodden got a little foxy and made a loop of paper or ribbon which they all signed and attached to the document, thus making it impossible to identify the order of the petitioners. The best laid plans, and all that. . . sometimes the king hanged the lot to make sure that he got the right one!

In the Britsh Navy, the sailors used the same device in petitions to the captain who, like the aforementioned kings, could hang the organiser on the grounds that his actions could be considered mutinous. By the time that the sailors had finished with the French term *rond ruban* – 'round ribbon', it had been bastardised to 'round robin'. More often than not, Navy round robins appeared with the signatures on the petition itself, but arranged in the form of a wheel with spokes. This, however, was far from foolproof, for one British captain, possessed of a malicious turn of wit, flogged all the men whose names made the spokes because they were the 'spokesmen'.

RUN THE GAUNTLET

Despite its seeming quite obvious, even apposite, there is no connection between this expression and the gauntlet as thrown down in challenge. Instead, this stands as one of the few examples of Swedish influence in current English phraseology, we having picked the term up from troops of that nation during the Thirty Years War.

Common to almost every culture is the form of punishment whereby the miscreant is obliged to run between two lines of men who are equipped with sticks or rope-ends and are intent on inflicting a certain amount of discomfort upon the unfortunate runner to whom the weight of the blows act as an accurate indication as to his popularity with his fellows. In the Swedish Army, this was a standard military field punishment and was known as the *gatlopp* – the run lane. When the word first appeared in English, it did so in the form of 'gantlope' and is still listed under such spelling in the OED.

SHOW OR SHAKE A LEG

Due to the fact that a high percentage of a man-of-war's crew were pressed men, captains were reluctant to grant shore leave since said men would most likely hightail it, never to be seen again. Because of this it was commonplace for women to be allowed to stay on board during a ship's stay in port, sometimes being permitted to remain when the vessel left. When it was time that all hands were on deck, the quarters would be checked by the boatswain who would cry, 'Show a leg!' to all still occupied hammocks. If it was obviously a woman's leg she was allowed to sleep on, but if it was a man's he was turfed out and put to work.

SIDEBURNS

General Ambrose Everett Burnside (1824–81) could not claim to have had a brilliant career in the Union Army during the American Civil War; to the Confederates he was something of a hero which just about sums up the man's tactical capabilities. One of his most inspired fiascos occurred when he decided to dynamite a trench along which his men could run into the midst of a Rebel stronghold without being fired on once. The explosives went off and his men dutifully charged down the trench only to find that they could not climb out at the other end, leaving the puzzled but grateful Confederates with hundreds of prisoners in an eight-foot deep pit. 'Only Burnside could have pulled off such a coup, wringing one last spectacular defeat from the jaws of victory' was Lincoln's comment when told of the event. Not long after, Burnside was replaced by General Hooker who gave his name to something far more interesting! (See under HOOKER in this section.)

Burnside's only significance, apart from his dazzling incompetence, was his enormous side-whiskers, leading them to being named after him. Because Burnside invariably got everything wrong and put the cart before the horse, it became the fashion in military circles to reverse his name and call them 'sideburns'.

SLUSH FUND

Navy cooks used to be able to make a bit on the side by saving up the fact derived from the boiling down of meats and selling it to the purser who, in turn, made it into candles and sold them to the sailors. Nobody made a fortune, but it was usually enough to fund a good binge in the next port of call. The fat was known as 'slush'.

SNOOKER

Not only is the name of military origin but so too is the actual game itself!

When serving in India in 1875, Col Sir Neville Chamberlain (no relation to Neville 'In my hand I have a piece of paper' Chamberlain) was stationed at Jubbulpore and, bored by all the existing table games, devised snooker by drawing on pool, pyramids and billiards. The name arose from a casual remark made by the game's creator when he and some fellow officers were playing the game.

Probably based on 'snooks', the nose-thumbing derisive gesture, the term 'snooker' had for some time been common in Army slang to describe a new cadet at the Royal Military Academy, Woolwich, many of whose alumni were at Jubbulpore. On the night in question, Chamberlain mocked an officer who failed to pot a ball that was hanging over a pocket by saying: 'Why, you're a regular snooker!' Several officers present were ignorant of the term's application and needed it explaining to them. Chamberlain is recorded as saying in a conversation many years later with Compton Mackenzie that, having explained his comment, he felt obliged to sooth the relevant officer's feathers by adding that, since the game itself was new, they were all 'snookers'.

SON OF A GUN

As explained in the entry under the heading SHOW A LEG, it was far from uncommon to find a few doxies on board a serving ship of the line. Since most such women were, shall we say, in the service industry, it was not unknown for them to fall pregnant and, sailors being sailors and doxies being doxies, paternity was at best a matter of conjecture. If a woman went into labour whilst on board, a make-shift screen was slung between two guns, which was the only place for her to get any privacy without blocking a gangway. Because of the aforementioned uncertainty of paternity, the birth was entered in the ship's log as 'son of a gun'.

STEAL A MARCH

Not unnaturally, this expression, meaning to gain an unexpected advantage over an opponent, derives from an army forcing the pace and marching through the night to arrive somewhere before the enemy expects them to.

SWASHBUCKLER

Perhaps Hollywood saved this word from extinction by producing films of the Errol Flynn genre *ad nauseam*. In sword fighting, 'swash' described a sweeping scyth-like blow, and a buckler was a little round shield. The more flamboyant swordsmen were often seen swashing their swords against their bucklers, which was probably not as painful as it sounds, in a display of bravado calculated to intimidate the enemy.

SWEET FANNY ADAMS

In 1820, a young girl named Fanny Adams was butchered in Hampshire by some lunatic, bits of her being found all over the place. This coincided with the first issues of tinned mutton to the Navy who, with typical forces humour, christened the new rations 'Fanny Adams'. After the press had dubbed the poor victim 'Sweet Fanny Adams', the sobriquet was adopted by the forces in general to stand for 'sweet fuck all' since, to put it crudely, that was all that was left of the girl in question.

TANK

Cumbersome and now laughably inefficient as the first tanks were, when the British first fielded them against the Germans in the First World War, large numbers of the Kaiser's finest suddenly found themselves remembering something that they just had to do on the other side of the battlefield. The machines were moved up to the front under cover and great secrecy by rail. All the attendant paperwork referred to the contents of the massive wooden crates as 'Bulk Water Carriers' and, because of this cover story, Sir Ernest Swinton, one of the leading figures in the development of such machines, began to refer to them as 'tanks' and the name just stuck.

TATTOO

In its military sense, this word first came into vogue in the mid seventeenth century in the Netherlands where British troops were on active duty during seemingly interminable squabbling with the Dutch. Due to the understandable hostility that Dutch civilians felt towards British troops in occupation of various areas of Dutch soil, it was considered wise to round all the men up, which basically meant clearing them out of the taverns, around nine at night to avoid unnecessary friction with the locals. A sort of 'last orders' drum squad used to march through the streets playing a distinctive beat that called for all beer sales to troops to cease and for the men to return to camp. *Taptoe* – that being the Dutch for 'the (beer) tap is shut' became corrupted to 'tattoo' by the troops. Traditionally, military extravaganzas are opened by a drum squad and wound up by the playing of that particular beat. The Americans, incidentally, were satisfied with the first part of the original Dutch which gave them 'taps' which is now mainly used at military funerals.

TELL IT TO THE MARINES

There are innumerable apocryphal stories attached to the origin of this expression. Invariably they are basically a roundabout compliment to that branch of the forces, so it can safely be assumed that the Marines themselves are the most likely authors attempting to cover up the truth. The usual story has Samuel Pepys regaling the court of Charles II with tales of wondrous sights that men had seen. When he mentioned what are commonly called 'flying' fish there was much scepticism but a Marine officer present chimed in that he too had seen them on a past voyage, whereupon the King supposedly launched himself upon the full sea of rambling dialogue about the Marines being the most widely travelled of any of his subjects, and that if they believed something then that was good enough for him. Unfortunately for credibility, this would give the expression the meaning of corroboration whereas it actually means 'I don't believe that' and, in truth, the saying is of naval origin and stems from the sailors' scorn for the Army whom they considered gullible enough to swallow anything.

THREE MILE LIMIT
With countries extending their claims to territorial waters every day, this no longer has any real application outside the old duty-free goodies. When it was set, many years ago, three miles was the maximum range of the old muzzle-loading shore batteries and was therefore the limit of the effective protection of any nation from its own soil.

TOMMY
The affectionate name applied by the British to the average soldier. It has been in fashion since 1815 when the first soldier's account books were issued. Every enlisted man was given one to keep records of the details of his service. The specimen form in the front showing him how to fill it in properly was completed in the hypothetical name of Thomas Atkins.

TROPHY
Today, trophies are something brought back and retained by the victor, but this was not always the case. The first trophies were built and left on the battlefield. The word stems from the Greek *trope* – a putting to flight – because the Greeks used to erect a small monument, usually made from the discarded arms of the

vanquished, on the precise spot where the turning point in the battle occurred.

TWENTY-ONE GUN SALUTE

An old Navy joke says that when the Queen has a baby they fire a twenty-one gun salute, but when a nun has one, they fire a dirty old canon. Be that as it may, the number is fixed at twenty-one because that was the number of guns carried on each side of the old ships of the line. The loading of the old guns was not the speediest of procedures, so to fire a broadside in salute which effectively disarmed the ship, was taken as the greatest mark of respect that a vessel could show in deference to another.

It was Samuel Pepys who worked out the number of guns to be used in the various salutes, moving upwards from three. The number of guns involved is always odd, since even numbers are fired at Navy funerals. Since the early guns had to be genuinely loaded to produce a suitable bang, it was not unknown for a polite gesture to spark off an incident through it being misconstrued.

UP THE SPOUT
As a less-than-charming way of describing one's para-mour after your combined passion has culminated in the anticipation of the patter of tiny feet, this developed in infantry slang where it initially applied to a rifle which was not only loaded but had a round in the breech ready to fire.

VIP
Towards the end of the last war, Transport Command was lumbered with the headache of moving a party of

very top brass, which counted amongst its number the late Lord Mountbatten. Security was, of course, at a maximum and the officer in charge of transporting this party to the Middle East in one piece, used the now familiar initials as a code name for his charges and for the operation in general.

SHIPPING AND TRANSPORT

A1

Commonly understood in all English-speaking countries, this expression was donated to the language by Lloyds Register of British and Foreign Shipping. This publication gives a rating to the world's shipping expressed in letters, which gave an indication as to the state of the hull, and numbers, which related to the condition of the vessel's equipment. As far as the shipping world is concerned, this designation is essentially obsolete today since it refers to ships with wooden hulls. The current equivalent for steel ships is 100A1.

ABACK – TO BE TAKEN

When a sailing vessel is hit by a squall of wind from the direction in which it is travelling, the sails, quite understandably, fall back against the mast and momentarily deprive the ship of all drive. The sensation experienced by those on board is something akin to travelling in a car when the driver brakes unexpectedly. Under such conditions, a ship is said to have been taken aback which explains the phrase's current employment.

ALL SHIP SHAPE AND BRISTOL FASHION

Throughout most of the great sail era, Bristol enjoyed a reputation for being the country's most efficient and orderly port. The days of sail may have faded, but that city's name lives on in English phraseology, albeit in application to things far removed from dockland efficiency.

ARGOSY

Increasingly heard in general usage to describe any sort of 'Aladdin's Cave', metaphorical or otherwise, this term properly applies to a type of merchantman that used to be built in and sailed from Ragusa in Dalmatia – that place being better known today as Dubrovnik. These ships, then called 'Ragusyes', were purpose built to carry large and varied cargoes.

ATLAS

One of the first milestones in navigation came in 1595 when the maps of Gerardus Mercator were published in a single volume by his son, Rumold. Sensitive to the fact that this was the first comprehensive work of its kind, in that it employed the Mercator Projection which enabled the maps to show the world as if flat, with all lines of longitude and latitude running parallel, but without distorting the navigational process, Mercator Jnr was anxious to produce a suitably impressive-looking book. In the end he went for the figure of Atlas, the Titan, supporting the world on his shoulders as a frontispiece. This had two effects: first, it ensured that all subsequent books of maps were called atlases and, secondly, it produced the myth that Atlas's punishment for fighting the gods of Olympus was supporting the world, whereas it was the heavens he was condemned to carry, the Atlas Mountains supposedly being his petrified remains.

BEAM ENDS – TO BE ON YOUR

This is really only the nautical equivalent of 'to be on your uppers'. In a ship, the beams are the heavy transverse timbers that run at right angles to the keel, so any vessel heeled over so hard that she was riding on her beam ends was in a great deal of trouble.

BETWEEN THE DEVIL AND THE DEEP BLUE SEA

There is no connection whatsoever between this expression and Old Nick. The devil in question is a seam in the hull of wooden sailing ships located near the waterways, so, if you found yourself between the devil and the deep blue sea then you had almost no room for manoeuvre.

It is often said that it was the ship's caulkers who gave that seam its peculiar name because gaining access to it to fill it with pitch was an extremely awkward procedure. But, given the knowledge of the deep blue hue of the usual expressions trotted out by irate matelots, the image of one of them turning to his workmates and saying something along the lines of, 'I say, this seam is the very Devil of a job to get at!' just doesn't ring true somehow.

BITTER END – THE
Although you would be forgiven for thinking so, bitter feeling has nothing to do with this. The 'bitter end' of a rope on a ship is that end attached to the 'bitts', which are securing posts on the deck. So, when a cable or rope is payed out to the bitter end, it is at its limit, as is a person who has reached the end of his tether.

BLUE PETER – TO HOIST THE
Saying that it is time that you hoisted the blue peter is a tongue-in-cheek way of saying that it is high time that you were leaving, since that is the flag raised by a ship to indicate her imminent departure. Actually, in pre-radio days the flag was used to ask another to repeat a message that had not been understood, its current name being a corruption of 'blue repeater'.

BY AND LARGE
No matter how sophisticated modern sail technology gets, no sailing ship is ever going to be able to sail fully into the wind. If, however, this is the desired direction, it

is necessary to assume a series of dog-legs to achieve the objective and, in sailing parlance, such tactics are known as 'sailing by and large' to the wind. The expression took on its present meaning to landlubbers because, whilst the ship is never actually pointed in the desired direction, it is travelling in the general direction of the required destination.

CHOCK-A-BLOCK
This can be briefly explained as it refers to the two parts of a block and tackle which, when fully hauled, are fast up against each other.

CLEAN BILL OF HEALTH
Before a ship can depart a port, that country's authorities must satisfy themselves that there are no cases of notifiable diseases on board. Having done so, they issue a clean bill of health which that ship's captain must produce at his next port of call.

CLEAN SLATE
As a common expression meaning a fresh start, this owes its existence to the log-slate as was once used to record the details of speeds and distances covered during a ship's watch. Prior to the one watch retiring and another taking over, all the notes on the slate would be entered up in the deck log, and the slate wiped clean for the new shift.

COPPER BOTTOMED
This is an old shipping insurance expression used to describe anything that was sure-fired. It alluded to the wooden-hulled ships that had been copper-clad to

protect themselves from all the obvious dangers that such vessels fell prone to. Naturally enough, as an insurance risk, they were a far better bet than unclad ships.

CUT AND RUN

Carrying heavy connotations of 'doing a bunk', this derives from the habit of captains who anticipated the need to depart hurriedly to avoid protracted and unseemly bickering with Excise men and the like over pettifogging technicalities to moor their ship in an open 'roadstream', or current, with the sails furled in such a way that, at the cut of a few well-placed restraining ties, they would fall into use almost immediately. It is sometimes asserted that the expression is born of ships cutting their anchor cables to effect a speedy departure, but this is not the case. Even when using the afore-mentioned trick, and many others, getting one of those cumbersome great things under way was slow even at its fastest, and there was always ample time to haul in the anchor – something that ships could hardly afford to leave behind, even if they were carrying a spare.

DAVY JONES'S LOCKER

This has long been sailors' slang for the bottom of the sea, a kind of hell for sailors to whom 'Fiddler's Green' was heaven; not the kind of heaven that you hear about from the clergy, more a sort of celestial knocking-shop.

In all honesty, no one knows where either of the expressions derive from. In the case of Davy Jones, the usual story put forward by some 'etymologists' cites a murderous pirate called Davy Jones, who had an obsessional predilection for making people walk the plank. Unfortunately, history does not make any mention of any such gentleman and, secondly, pirates did not make people walk the plank; being somewhat unsubtle fellows, if they wanted you off the ship, they just pushed you over the side or, if you were unlucky enough to be caught by the Caribbean branch of the scrofulous brotherhood, you might be attached to a rope and given a worm's-eye view of shark fishing.

There have been some more sophisticated attempts to explain the name by asserting it to be an amalgam of 'Duffy' – a West Indian sea-devil, and 'Shonee' – a Celtic sea-god. Jonah of biblical whale fame has also been dragged in from time to time but, at the end of the day, it's most likely just a name picked at random for no good reason.

THE DEVIL TO PAY

There is a double misconception locked up in the expression in the heading because, not only is the 'devil' not Satan, but 'pay' is not the same word as used in the sense of restitution.

As with the saying 'between the devil and the deep blue sea', the 'devil' mentioned is a seam bordering the waterways on the hull of wooden ships. It was significantly larger than most of the others and therefore required more pitch than usual to seal it. 'Pay', in this context, is derived from the French verb *peier* which means to cover with pitch. The original and full expression, which was born in the shipyards of yester-day, was 'there's the devil to pay and no hot pitch', which gives the saying the real meaning of an awkward situation with no apparent solution. Because of the popular misconception surrounding the expression, it is invariably applied in completely the wrong context, namely, that since a terrible mistake has been made, great trouble will follow and the Devil will want his due – 'there'll be the Devil to pay for this', is the usual format.

FALL FOUL

Yet again of seafaring origin, to a sailor this can mean one of two things, both of which are in keeping with the saying's current usage. A ship is said to have fallen foul of another if that second ship precedes it in a shipping lane at a slower pace and there is no room to 'overtake'. The secondary meaning describes an anchor which, when drawn in, is found to have got caught up in its own cable.

FLOTSAM AND JETSAM

On land, this enjoys only metaphorical employment, usually in application to a motley bunch of undesirables. At sea, however, the words have quite precise meanings. The former designates goods lost at sea which continue to float, and the latter goods deliberately tossed over the side in an attempt to lighten the vessel and reduce the risk of sinking. Actually, it is from such justifiable practice that we get our word 'average'. In the event of such taking place, and the vessel surviving as a result, the cost of the jettisoned goods is divided up evenly between the owners of the other shipments on board that were saved. The marine insurance term for such division of loss was 'general average', 'average' having been previously used in medieval days to describe the expected amount of work that a serf would get through in one day. Quite how it made the massive side-step to shipping insurance nobody knows.

There is another classification apart from flotsam and jetsam, and that is 'lagan'. Nothing like so widely known as the other two, this applies to goods thrown overboard but attached to a marker so that they could be picked up later.

GONE BY THE BOARDS

In the 'Don't put your daughter on the stage, Mrs Worthington!' days, when the term 'actress' carried the same sort of euphemistic connotations as does 'exotic dancer' today, there were attempts to explain this expression by saying that it referred to 'fallen' women who had gone to 'tread the boards'. A nice try, but not so. The boards in question are those that make up the clinker of a ship's hull, and the expression quite simply refers to things thrown into the sea.

HACKNEY AND HACK

Haquenée was an old French word applied to an ambling horse, or one of a less-than-spirited nature. Since no one with any brains would have rented out a fine animal, because it would have been treated much the same as a hire-car is today, the term transferred to the plodding type of nag that one would expect to emerge from a rental stable. Usually worked to death, these animals were tired and played out before their time, which is why the word spread to encompass anything tired and repetitive, especially writers.

HALF SEAS OVER

Admittedly one of the less common expressions to describe someone who has enjoyed a surfeit of alcohol, but it is still heard. In a bad storm, a ship can heel over so far that the sea covers half her decks. If you have ever seen men staggering around under such dangerous conditions, you will remember that they move as if half-cut, tottering from side to side like drunks.

HARD AND FAST

Quite simply, this refers to a ship that has run aground and is stuck fast. The expression 'hard up', as in penniless, originally applied to a ship swung fully round to bring her head directly into the wind, in which position she was in dire difficulty.

HOBSON'S CHOICE

Essentially this means having no choice at all and derives from the name of a once nationally famous Cambridge-based haulage contractor who was also the owner of the largest stock of horses for hire in the area. Thomas Hobson (1544–1631) was renowned for his meticulous rotation of the animals for hire; if an animal had been out to work on one day, then it rested the next, no matter who wanted to hire it. When you went to Hobson to hire a horse, you got the animal whose turn it was to go, there was no question of taking your pick of the stable.

Although he sounds very much like an apocryphal character, he is actually mentioned by Milton in two works and in issue no. 509 of the *Spectator* (14.10.1712) for donating a conduit structure to the city's market.

HUNKY DORY

In 1854, Commodore Perry visited Japan and secured trade agreements that led to American merchantmen making Yokohama a regular port of call. The main street leading away from the docks was called Huncho dori and it contained many bars and other establishments of great interest to sailors on shore leave. Since everything that they could possibly want was on the same street, there was no risk of getting lost and, when appetites had been sated, hopefully without picking up a dose of the local culture, all they had to do was stagger back to the ship. In its altered form of 'hunky dory' the term was not widely used until a song made popular later during the Civil War by the original Christy Minstrels. Entitled 'Josephus Orange Blossom' and containing the line 'red-hot hunky dory contraband', the song was 'top of the pops' throughout the conflict.

JERRY BUILT

The usual story attached to this is that it derives from the fact that the walls of Jericho supposedly tumbled down when Joshua and his merry men gave an impromptu concert for the city's defenders. This, and a couple of digs at the Germans, can safely be discounted. 'Jerry' is a corruption of 'jury', as in the maritime expression 'jury built' which was a tag for any repairs done in a hurry with whatever was to hand. This could be anything from patching up storm damage to rigging a temporary mast. Naturally enough, some of the repairs were pretty Heath Robinson and did not always last until port. As for the derivation of the word 'jury' itself, that seems to come from the old French *ajurie* which meant relief.

JUGGERNAUT

A corruption of the name of Jagannath, one of the Krishna reincarnations of Vishnu and a supreme god of the Hindu Trimurti. It is traditional for a massive idol of the god to be dragged through the streets of Puri in eastern India, as a means of transferring the god to his summer residence. A cart of staggering proportions is used for the purpose and a myth has grown up over the centuries that the demented faithful used to toss themselves under the wheels to be crushed to death and thus released from the unending circle of life and rebirth. There have been a number of deaths over the years, but these have resulted from crowd pressure rather than by fanatics electing to rush rudely unannounced into the presence of their creator.

LET FLY
When coming into harbour in a small, single-sail craft, the unwise and the flashy are wont to let go, or let fly, the ropes that restrain the bottom edge of the sail; a sort of unprofessional seaman's version of switching off the car engine and allowing the vehicle to coast to a halt. This is fine unless something untoward happens, because all drive disappears with the release of that rope, as does a large percentage of the manoeuvrability of the craft.

LIMOUSINE
Today's plush pose-mobiles owe their name to the distinctive type of hooded garment that was once traditional dress in Limousin in the French Massif Central. When the first private automobiles emerged in France, equipped with a hooded passenger compartment, but with the poor old driver exposed to the elements, they were nicknamed 'limousines' in allusion to the hoods worn by the people of Limousin.

LOG OF A SHIP
In the days before sophisticated navigation and modern sail technology which allows ships to go in directions other than that in which the wind happens to be blowing at the time, there wasn't much to record in the vessel's diary except details of speed and distance made over a specific period. Since these figures were arrived at by the high-tech method of throwing a log over the side, which subsequently dragged out a knotted rope at a given 'rate of knots', the record book became known as

the log book and speed was thereafter expressed in knots.

PANTECHNICON

The abysmal failure of a nineteenth-century venture into the arts is behind this lofty term for the humble furniture van.

In 1830, a group of businessmen and art experts got together to build a massive emporium for every imaginable art form. The building, located just off Belgrave Square in Motcomb Street, was named The Pantechnicon, which is Greek for 'belonging to all the arts'. It was an unqualified failure and the place was sold off to a removal and storage company, Londoners wryly applying the old arty name to the vans of the new business.

PLAIN SAILING

In 1569, Gerardus Mercator produced the first navigation charts incorporating his now famous Mercator Projection. Without going into too much detail, what the man had managed to do was to show sections of the earth's surface as if flat, overlay this with a grid of the lines of longitude and latitude drawn as running straight, parallel and intersecting at right angles, yet without distorting the navigational process. These 'plane charts', as they were popularly known, made a ship's navigator's job much simpler. Now he could plot a course as if the ship was actually moving across a flat, or plane, surface. Without the constant need for correctional calculations, his job was therefore made 'plane sailing', this being the proper spelling of the expression.

PLIMSOLLS

A champion of the cause for better conditions for British seamen, Samuel Plimsoll fought a six-year battle to secure legislation to govern just how much a ship could carry. In 1876, he won his case and saved a good many men going to their deaths because of greed and short-sighted stupidity on behalf of the owners. Before long, every ship had to have a set of white lines painted on the bows and, when the first white canvas shoes emerged in the late 1920's, they picked up the nickname because they reminded people of the Plimsoll lines on the ships.

SHANKS'S PONY

In Old English, the tibia, the bone that is the major of the two connecting the knee and the ankle, was known as the *sceanca* – a name that later became modernised to 'shank'. In country districts, a thin, gangling person is still referred to as a 'spindleshanks'. Thus, to go by Shanks's pony is to travel on foot.

SOS

It is presumably unnecessary to state that the above does not stand for 'Save our Souls', '. . . Skins', '. . . Sausages', or any other of the more colourful, not to mention indecent, alternatives. Strangely enough, it does not even stand for the three letters, 'S', 'O' and 'S'.

Prior to 1908, when SOS was adopted as the official international distress signal, CQD had been in service. CQ on its own meant 'stand by to receive transmission', and the letter 'D' was added to indicate distress – not that this saved the signal from the tortured minds of erstwhile acronymaniacs, who promptly started spreading the story that the signal stood for 'Come Quick – Distress'. Anyway, the new signal was chosen, not because it spelled or represented anything, but because it was eminently memorable, recognisable and transmittable, even by a total novice such as a ship's passenger. Had it meant nothing at all in Morse, it would still have been chosen. It is transmitted as a pattern, not a sequence of letters.

The only distress call that does have any etymological story to tell is the verbal 'May Day' which is a corruption of the French *M'aidez!* which means 'Come and help me!'

SPICK AND SPAN

Dating from the early shipbuilding yards, this originally meant something more akin to 'brand new' than to neat and tidy. 'Spick' was an old variant of 'spike', as in nail, and 'span' an early word for a woodchip or shaving. The allusion was to a new ship with all the nails still shiny and her timbers still showing the marks of the carpenter's tools.

STARBOARD, LARBOARD AND PORT

Prior to the employment of 'port' and 'starboard', the seemingly lunatic choice of 'starboard' and 'larboard' had been in vogue for many a year. One would be forgiven for thinking that after the first time a cry of 'Hard a'larboard!' was misheard in a storm by a helmsman heading a vessel towards a danger intended to be avoided, sailors might 'have begun to suspect that having two such similar words for the two most vital commands aboard a ship was not such a good idea after all. Not a bit of it! Suicidally conservative, Britain did not officially adopt the new-fangled 'port' until 1844 — mainly as a result of the efforts of Rear-Admiral Robert Fitzroy who, in his youth, had captained the brig *Beagle*, aboard which Charles Darwin sailed into controversy.

In the days before centralised rudders, sea-going ships

used a long oar over the right-handed side of the stern, and it is from this that the word 'starboard' derives, not from any fanciful idea that star bearings were always taken from the right-hand side of the ship. 'Star' is a variant of 'stear', which was the Anglo-Saxon for 'to steer'. In an attempt to reduce the risk of the steerage gear becoming fouled with debris floating in the ports, a ship would always tie up with the left-hand side against the dock. As a direct result of this, the cargo was always loaded on to the left or 'ladeboard' side; this later corrupting to 'larboard' before changing to 'port'.

SWING THE LEAD

Without doubt, the most pleasant and desirable job on any sailing vessel has to be what is known colloquially as 'swinging the lead'. Properly designated 'depth sounding', this entailed sitting at the prow of a ship and dropping a weighted and calibrated line over the side to assess draught when negotiating shallow waters. What a lovely way to pass a day! Not unnaturally, all the other hands who were still charging round the decks eyed the tranquil figure of their 'workmate' with much jealousy.

Although it has got nothing to do with this expression, it is worth mentioning that it was from similar practice on the Mississippi river boats that the writer Samuel Langhorne Clemens got his pen-name of Mark Twain. The depthline only had three marks on it, upper, twain and lower. When the sounder called 'Mark twain!' to the pilot, it indicated a safe two fathoms.

THREE SHEETS IN THE WIND

To explain this expression, meaning drunk, it must first be stated that, for reasons best known to themselves, this nation's jolly Jack Tars mean a rope, not a sail, when they say 'sheet', especially the restraining ropes attached to the bottom of a sail. When a rope is slackened off completely, it is said to be 'in the wind', and particularly on a small craft, if all three restraining sheets on the sails are slackened off, the sails flap uncontrollably and the craft drifts.

UNDER THE WEATHER
When inexperienced sailors suddenly assume a Robespierre-like complexion and go scurrying down into the bowels of the ship to call for God on the big white telephone, not only are they feeling a trifle under the weather, but that is literally where they are headed – whence the origin of the expression.

POLITICS AND RELIGION

AMBITION

Just what every 'upwardly mobile' political animal needs by the bucketful if he is going to be successful. It was the Romans who coined this word for political aspirants who, due to the lack of more sophisticated forms of mass communication, had to wander round grabbing people by the togas and chat them up in an attempt to secure their vote or support. 'Ambition' is built on *ambitio* which meant to go wandering about.

ASSASSIN

If you are a famous politician, it must, in these troubled times, be of great comfort to know that you cannot be murdered, only assassinated. Quite what comfort this banal exercise in semantics is to you after you have been shot is not easy to estimate, but there it is for what it is worth. Perhaps it is just another facet of the intricate class structure in this country that only commoners get murdered. All that aside, the word was introduced into English by returning Crusaders. The word is an Anglicised form of *Hashishin*, that translating as 'hashish-eater' and being the name of a sect of fanatical Isma'ili Moslems who, like all good religious extremists, worked on the tried and trusted principle that the best way to prove their own brand of the truth, was to kill those who did not agree with it. Perhaps it was ironically fitting that it was the Crusaders who brought the word home!

BACKSTAIRS INFLUENCE

As a term for the unseen and invariably sinister sway held over a governing body, this alludes to the royal courts of old where, if one courtier wanted to see someone that he would rather not be seen seeing, he would sneak to that person's room by the backstairs used by the servants.

BANDWAGGON – TO CLIMB ON THE

American politics have always been the undignified, gaudy circus-type affairs that they are today. In the days before the dubious bounties of television and mass media, the first thing that a candidate would do upon arriving at a town was to hire a waggon large enough to accommodate himself, his entourage and a small band, whose job it was to play through the streets and attract attention because, let's face it, everybody loves a parade. Any local figures who felt so inclined could climb onto the waggon as it moved through the town, thus indicating to the locals their support for the candidate. This could go a long way to securing votes – a favour which was expected to be returned should the man attain office. Since most of the lesser local figures would most often wait for a lead from the more prominent ones, the expression took on its unsavoury overtones.

BOYCOTT

In 1880, one Captain Charles Cunningham Boycott was the land agent in County Mayo for the estates of the Earl of Erne, and, all in all, his approach to land management made Rachman look like an officer from 'Shelter'. He was a natural choice to be a target for Parnell's movement which urged tenants to sever all contact with unjust and oppressive landlords. No labour, no supplies, no mail delivered, no contact of any kind at all!

Despite labour being brought in from Northern Ireland under military guard, the Boycotts eventually had to admit defeat and return to England where they were welcomed as heroes.

BREAK A LEG!

One of the many peculiarities of the acting profession is their somewhat unique way of wishing each other good luck with a performance. The expression rose from, of all things, the assassination of President Lincoln by John Wilkes Booth who was by trade an actor. After killing his victim Booth paused to indulge in theatricals by mounting the edge of the Presidential box and proclaiming to a stunned audience, 'Thus ever to tyrants!' — which he said in Latin for additional effect. Having left the vast majority of the non-classically educated audience puzzling as to just what it was that he was raving about, Booth did a Douglas Fairbanks down to the stage, but ruined the whole effect by fracturing his leg on landing and had to exit stage-left at an undignified hobble, totally botching his entire performance.

BRINKMANSHIP

This emerged in 1956 when it was used in a speech by Adlai Stevenson to describe the 'policies' of the then Secretary of State, J. Foster Dulles, one of the greatest liberal minds since Attila the Hun. Dulles was inflexibly opposed to talks with the Russians on any subject, American recognition of Communist China, and so on, and it was felt, in some quarters, that such policies were taking America to the brink of all out war with the Communists.

Several years later, when the word was in fairly common use, Stevenson was asked about its invention. He was of the opinion that, although everyone attributed it to him, he only used it having heard it somewhere, sometime.

BUGGER

A strange term to arise from religious sectarian bickering but, nevertheless, that's where it comes from.

In the south of France of the twelfth century, there were large numbers of adherents to Manichean teachings, which were a little sceptical about the content of the gospels, and were not altogether convinced that Jesus had been the Son of God. Now, that may be all very well today, especially with the Bishop of Durham taking pot-shots at his own sacred cows, but holding opinions that were in conflict with the Vatican at that time was conviction of a terminal nature. Being a good Christian, Pope Innocent III decided that he'd better kill the lot of them – so he did! Since the sect had strong associations with the Bulgarian Bogamils, the French *Bougre* – Bulgarian – lived on after they had been massacred, as a term of abuse to describe a heretic believed capable of any vice, especially sodomy. By the time that the word arrived in English, it had altered in spelling, lost all religious overtones, and went to enrich the considerable English arsenal of obscenities.

BUNK

In 1820, the American House of Representatives was engaged in debating the Missouri Compromise; they wanted that state in the Union but it was still a slave-state so some way round this minor technicality had to be found. In the middle of this debate, there rose to speak a certain Felix Walker, Congressman for Buncombe County, North Carolina. Having either been asleep for the previous few hours or overdoing the fire-water, Walker proceeded to deliver a speech that was as protracted as it was totally unrelated to the matter under discussion. In response to the jeers and cries of, 'I say, for heaven's sake sit down, old chap!', or words to such effect, Walker imperiously replied: 'Your insults are of no consequence. I am not speaking for your ears, but for Buncombe's.' The county name later became bastardised to 'bunkum' before getting cut in half.

CANDIDATE

Although the term's use is by no means restricted to that of the political application, this is where the etymological roots lead. In ancient Rome, it was the habit of those running for public office to dress up in white robes to indicate the purity of their intentions to the electorate. If the average Roman swallowed all this, he certainly got the government he deserved! The Latin for being dressed in white was *candidatus*.

CARNIVAL

Properly this applies to the three days preceding Lent which were given over to general self-indulgence and feasting in order to build up body reserves for the self-denial and fasting of Lent proper. No fools, these early Christians! The word is built on two Latin ones, *carnis* and *levare*, which mean 'flesh' and 'to put away' respectively, for, when the period of Carnival was over, there was an absence of meat. Fairly obviously, 'carnival' is therefore a sister-word of 'carnage', even 'carnal' and, less obviously, 'carnation', a flower named for its flesh-coloured petals.

CARPETBAGGER

This Americanism has a precise meaning of a candidate standing in a constituency where he does not reside.

After the end of the American Civil War, the bankrupted South was flooded with get-rich-quick speculators from the North intent on buying up plantations and businesses at toy-town prices. Travelling light and fast, these men were recognisable by their large, almost Gladstone bag-shaped travelling-grips made of strong carpet material. Following in their wake was a massive influx of Northern officials and politicians to take control of the Southern administration. They were soon saddled with the nickname 'carpetbaggers' themselves.

CATHERINE WHEEL

This ever popular firework is named after St Catherine of Alexandria who, like so many other saints, was probably no more than myth and tradition. The list of such saints grew alarmingly over the centuries until, in 1969, the Vatican decided to weed out from its honours list those saints of dubious existence. Out went Christopher, our very own George, and Vitus, the patron saint of disco-dancers, to name but a few.

The Catherine in question here was supposedly a lady of quality in Alexandria during the reign of the pagan Maxentius – or Maximinus. Tradition has it that having failed to shift her from her Christian beliefs, the Emperor had her flogged and then broken on the wheel, or at least he tried to have her broken on the wheel, for every time the soldiers tried to fix her to it, it rolled away. When they succeeded, the wheel simply shattered and killed many spectators with its debris.

CHANGING HORSES IN MID-STREAM

It was President Lincoln who first used this; whether he 'invented' it or it was a legacy from his backwoods days is unclear, but it was he who put the saying into circulation. He slipped it into a speech in which he was making light of his renomination for the Presidency by the Republicans by saying that his party had most likely decided it unwise to change horses in mid-stream, referring metaphorically to himself as the horse and the Civil War as the river.

CHAPEL
Oddly enough, this derives from the Latin *capella* which translates as 'a little cloak'. The reason for this dates back to the Franks, when no royal entourage would dream of moving without carting along a small shrine containing the cloak that supposedly belonged to St Martin. Later the word spread to include any depository of relics, whose guardians were called *capellanus* – whence our word 'chaplain'.

CHEAT
How appropriate it is that this word is derived directly from a former title of officers of the Exchequer! The 'Escheators' of old were men sent in to manage estates that fell forfeit to the Crown or to feudal lords due to failure of the heirs to qualify, there being no heir at all, or for reasons of treason or felony. The notorious and wholesale fiddling that these fellows got up to ensured that the altered form of their title went down in history as a tribute to their corruption and greed.

CONCLAVE
Following the death of a Pope, the Cardinals are faced with the task of deciding who is to put on the shoes of the fisherman. The rooms to which they retire to thrash the matter out (sometimes quite literally, in the old days!) are all fitted with the same lock, and are therefore accessible by the one key. Because of this the Conclave gets its name, from the Latin *cum* and *clavis* which mean 'together' and 'key'. Nowadays, the term has a far more general meaning, it being applied to any ecclesiastical meeting of importance.

CORRIDORS OF POWER

As a collective term for the anonymous bodies infested by hordes of little grey men who control our lives from behind closed doors, this is something of a cliché these days. It first appeared in a novel by C. P. Snow entitled *Homecomings* and caught on so rapidly that he used it as a title for a later novel in 1964.

CRETIN

Cretinism is a condition of mental deficiency caused by malfunction of the thyroid gland and the endemic form is to be found in central Switzerland and the Pyrenees. 'Cretin' is an anglicised form of the name given to the unfortunate sufferers in the Pyrenees – *Chretien*, which actually meant 'Christian'. You see, most cultures explained away their lunatics by putting the condition down to the touch of the hand of God, which made the mental defectives blessed in their innocence. Quite why people should choose to blame God is unclear, but the notion was not lacking in this country either; the expression claiming that someone is 'a bit touched' is evidence enough of that.

CURATE'S EGG

This, meaning a mixture of good and bad, was born out of a cartoon that appeared in the magazine, *Punch*, in 1895. The picture was of a young and very obviously nervous curate breakfasting with his bishop whom he is frightened of offending by complaining that his egg is off. When asked by his superior if the egg is to his liking, he replies: 'Parts of it are excellent.'

DEVIL'S ADVOCATE

This has its roots in the papal courts that sit to elect saints. Once a candidate's name has got as far as being presented to this court, it is highly unlikely that refusal is on the cards and the proceedings are a mere formality. Nevertheless, tradition decrees that as a safeguard there must be, as in any other court, someone attacking the motion from any and every possible angle just for the hell of it, for want of a better expression! Instead of defence and prosecution, there is the Devil's Advocate and God's Advocate, the former opposing the motion even though he is fully in favour of the proposed canonisation.

DOMINOES

As for the game, this was introduced into England around the middle of the eighteenth century by French POWs. The name, on the other hand, has a holy background for it is based on the Latin *Dominus* – 'God'. 'Domino' first appeared in eighteenth-century France as a term for the hood with eye-slits worn by priests in winter, the gaming tablets being so named in allusion to the whites of the wearer's eyes against the black background.

DUNCE

John Duns Scotus was one of the most respected scholars of the Middle Ages and, as a Franciscan philosopher, he was bitterly opposed to the theological changes advocated by Thomas Aquinas. He was not alone in this opposition and attracted a large following known as *Dunses*. Unfortunately for the memory of their leader, they carried on the good fight for 200 years after the man's death by which time the moderate changes that had taken place were a bit old hat and everybody regarded the Dunses as a bunch of blockheads.

DYED IN THE WOOL

In its political application, this refers to someone who is absolutely rigid of standpoint to the point of being dangerously brittle. It stems from the wool trade where it was known that yarn dyed before the make-up of a garment held its colour firmer than woollen garments dyed to the desired colour after manufacture.

FABIAN SOCIETY

This rather élite Socialist society that was formed in the winter of 1883, took its name, strangely enough, from one of the less socially oriented Roman generals, Quintus Fabius Maximus. Fabius it was who was sent to deal with the problem of Hannibal, whom he never actually engaged in battle. Instead he harassed his adversary, constantly snapping at his heels only to retreat; constantly · manoeuvring Hannibal into hilly terrain where his cavalry was less than useless; constantly wearing down Hannibal's army and supplies.

Until his strategy proved successful, Fabius got a lot of stick back in Rome, everyone being of the opinion that it was high time he stopped pussy-footing around and gave the barbarian the good solid seeing-to that he deserved. The Senate even started calling him *Cunctator* – 'The Delayer'. At the end of the day, such tactics proved valid and Fabius retained the slur Cunctator as a badge of honour and as a 'thumb to the nose' to everyone who had pilloried him before. When the Socialist society was formed, they turned their backs on all the Trots and hardline lefties, preferring instead to avoid revolution and bring about the desired social changes by a slow process of reasoning and education of governments and people alike.

FASCISM

Although this term is bandied about, tagged on to any old right-wing party, it only properly applies to the specific movement started by Benito Mussolini in the March of 1919.

What Mussolini was drawing on was the symbol of power carried by officials in Rome during its heyday. A *fasces* was a bundle of long birch rods with an axe-head sticking out from the middle. In an attempt to conjure up an image of the glory that once was, he resurrected the symbol and named his party after it.

FINE ITALIAN HAND

This was originally the formal description of the highly distinctive handwriting style of the scribes and secretaries of the Vatican. With all the murder, intrigue and double-dealing that went on in that stronghold of Christian virtue, it soon came to mean underhand tactics.

FOOLS PARADISE

Unwilling to appear unduly harsh on lunatics and simpletons, Mother Church, in her bountiful wisdom, decided that they didn't really deserve to burn in Hell because they had never been admitted to the Church, through no fault of their own. Since they could in no way be let into heaven, drooling all over the place, something had to be done. The solution was easy — invent another place for them to go to. Fool's Paradise, which was suitably located on the borders of Hell, not heaven, was the answer.

GABERDINE

Difficult though it may be to associate the old-type school raincoat with pilgrims, that is where the material derived its name! In the Middle Ages, when anyone who was anyone was going on pilgrimages like some people run marathons today, a good, hard-wearing cloak was an absolute must. This type of heavy diagonal twill was the answer to their prayers and, overnight, it became what the well-dressed pilgrim about town should wear. Because of this strong association, the French named the cloth *gauvardine* – pilgrimage.

GAUDY

Ultimately derived from the Latin *gaudium*, meaning 'joy', this is a classic example of a word that started life with great religious significance, only to end up meaning cheap and flashy. (*See also* TAWDRY.)

In the Middle Ages, a gaud was one of the major beads in a rosary. There were so many prayers that the faithful were expected to say in the course of a day that rosaries came into being to help people remember and count them off. Just to digress for a minute, the very word 'bead' used to mean a prayer and, with the advent of rosaries and the passage of time, the word moved from describing the prayer to the item that represented it on a rosary. However, that's by the way. The gauds were the larger beads placed to mark the end of the various sections. On expensive rosaries sported by the nobility, these did tend to be a bit ornate and conspicuous, sometimes even downright gaudy.

GERRYMANDERING

A lovely sounding word that describes the altering of electoral boundaries to ensure the continuance in power of the governing party. The word came into existence after one Elbridge Gerry (1744–1814), Governor of Massachusetts, indulged in such practices to make sure that his party retained certain marginal seats in forthcoming elections.

Now, this is not the sort of thing that can be carried out secretly, people tend to get a trifle suspicious if they go to bed in one county only to wake up in another, and loudest of the critics was the *Boston Sentinel*. Stuart, the resident cartoonist, produced some provisional drawings at an editor's meeting, one of which was taking the mickey out of the new boundary of Essex County. Gerry's new county shape reminded Stuart for all the world of a salamander — so he drew it as one. Benjamin Russell, the editor, suggested that Stuart redrew the cartoon with the face of the creature a caricature of Gerry and call it a Gerrymander. This he did, and that was that!

GIDDY
In Old English, *gidig* meant 'god possessed'. A lot of the early pagan rites included wild, uncontrollable dancing and whirling about. This invariably resulted in the 'congregation' getting dizzy and falling over, a phenomenon explained away by their priests as the spirit of whoever or whatever entering their bodies.

GOSSIP
Yet another religious word fallen from grace! *Godsibb*, as the word used to appear, described a godparent, *sibb* meaning kin or relative. Then, as now, visits from such 'relatives' are not the most frequent of affairs so, when they did occur, there was a lot of news to catch up on and a lot of 'godsibbing' took place around the fire.

HEATHEN
The contrast between the city dweller and the rustic was infinitely sharper in the old days. Most towns and cities

were fairly civilised oases amidst a dark, semi-pagan desert whose occupants were still leaping about in goatskins, jibbering and rolling their eyes every time something went bump in the night. It was because of this that the occupants of the erstwhile enclaves of Christian civilisation in England viewed his country cousins with a not altogether unfounded suspicion, and words like 'heathen', which is based on 'heath', bear witness to this feeling. 'Pagan', which is derived from *paganus*, the Latin for a rustic person, is but another example.

HIP! HIP! HURRAH!

The old and admittedly fanciful notion is that this derives from the Crusades when it was a battle-cry of the Christian knights who were busy slaying the infidel. Although it sounds a trifle contrived, it is not beyond the realms of possibility that 'Hip' is an acronym of *Hierosolyma est perdita*, 'Jerusalem is destroyed', destroyed in the sense of lost to the infidel; the original form of the cry was 'Hep' and not 'Hip'. As for 'Hurrah', the theory continues to postulate that this was a contribution from the Slavonic knights in that *hu-raj* in their language meant 'paradise'. If the theory is correct, the cry would therefore hold a meaning of 'Jerusalem has been saved from the infidel and we are on the road to paradise'.

HOCUS-POCUS

One of the early Church's best weapons for holding sway over the great unwashed, was the way that they muttered away in Latin so that no one in the congregation had the foggiest notion of what was being said. This added to the pseudo-mystique of the proceedings, not to mention reinforcing the idea that the clergy were somehow apart from the rest of humanity. In the consecration of the mass, the priests were always muttering *Hoc est corpus* – 'This is my body', and it was this that was picked on and bastardised to produce 'hocus-pocus'. Its current use was fixed forever when the expression was adopted by conjurers and magicians of old, to add to their repertoire of dog-Latin.

IN-LAWS
Contrary to popular opinion, the law referred to is not national legislation, but canon law which, amongst other things, lays down the guidelines and degrees of family relationship within which marriage is permitted.

IOTA – IT DOES NOT MATTER ONE
In the fourth century, a chap named Arius provoked what became known as the Arian Controversy which became the great talking point at cocktail parties throughout the Byzantine Empire. The orthodox Catholic standpoint was that God the Father and God the Son were one and the same, whereas Arius reckoned that, whilst they were similar, they were different. In Greek, the term for the doctrine that towed the party line was *Homo-ousion*, and for that of Arius it was *Homoi-ousion*. To the average Byzantian, totally unconcerned with purist theological controversy, it did seem to be something of a fuss about nothing, there being but one 'i' – termed *iota* in Greek – in the difference between their names; and what did one iota matter? The orthodox tolerated the wrangle for a short time before resorting to the tried and true tactic of declaring the other doctrine to be heretical and, being rather attached to their heads and being possessed of a strong aversion to being burnt alive, most of its followers lost interest in Arius and his silly ideas overnight.

LIFE BEGINS AT FORTY

Girls who were chosen to become Vestal Virgins were picked at the age of 10. Under pain of death they had to remain chaste throughout their service. At the age of 40 they were offered the opportunity of being released from their vows so that they could leave and marry if they so wished. Despite this seeming to have given rise to the expression, few ever did take the offer up, most preferring to retain their rank and privilege rather than trade all that in for the bitter fruits that they had lived thus far without. Besides, to be honest, a woman of 40 years in those days was not exactly the hottest prospect on the marriage market.

LIMBO

Being the ablative singular of the Latin *limbus*, meaning a fringe or border, 'Limbo' was yet another 'Heaven in Hell' invented by the medieval Church to tidy away the problem of what to do with all the souls of those who had died before the coming of Christ, still-born babies and those unbaptised before death. As when confronted with the headache of idiots and simpletons, the Church suddenly 'discovered' the very place for such unfortunates – Limbo, so named because it was on the borders of Hell. Since anyone sent there had to hang around until the Day of Judgement before they could get into Heaven proper, the word 'limbo' entered general usage with its present meaning.

THE MOUNTAIN TO MOHAMMED...

As did the Jews with Jesus, the Arabs were forever asking Mohammed to pull some miracle or other out of the turban to prove his power. To shut them up, the Prophet ordered Mount Safa to come to him, something that the mountain showed a marked reluctance to do.

Mohammed then told his flock of Doubting Dervishes that they should be damn glad that the mountain had not come or it would have crushed them to death and they jolly well ought to follow him up the mountain and offer thanks to Allah for the miraculous way that they had all been saved from a horrible death. Sounds like a man who would have had a bright career in politics.

MUD – HIS NAME IS

Having been successful in his bid to murder President Lincoln (*see also* under **Break a Leg!** in this section), Booth, who injured his leg during his escape from the theatre, took himself off to one Dr Sam Mudd, with whom he had a nodding acquaintance, to get some treatment. Mudd was subsequently arrested on charges of complicity and sent away for a very long time. Whether or not he had any knowledge of the plot has never been established either way. He claimed total ignorance of the President's death at the time of tendering what he thought was treatment for a riding accident, or so he claimed, but, on the other side of the coin, he lied about having met Booth several times, the last of which was in a hotel room with several other men, supposedly for a business meeting about the purchase of some land.

The expression 'his name is mud' had enjoyed limited circulation before the event mentioned above. It emanated from that sector of the press better known today as the 'Tit 'n Bum Beanos', but was originally called in America 'The Mud Press', from the old maxim, 'Throw enough mud and some of it is bound to stick'. However, thanks to the peculiar name of the good doctor who, incidentally, finally received a full pardon for having successfully fought an epidemic of yellow fever in the prison in which he was being held, the saying really took off and became so widespread that it soon crossed the Atlantic.

N OR M

As used when discussing something or someone who could be one thing or the other, this could derive from the first question of the Church of England Catechism, in response to which the questionee must reply with their name or names which, in Latin, is *nomen vel nomina*. In Latin, the usual way of writing what would be shown today as 'n's', to stand as an abbreviated form of 'names', was the double letter, 'nn', which, needless to say, could be and often was mistaken for the letter 'm'. Alternatively, it could just as well derive from the documentation and banns for marriage wherein the bride and groom are simply referred to as 'N' and 'M' as an abbreviation of *maritus* – bridegroom and *nupta* – the bride.

NINE DAY WONDER

Back in the good old days when God was for sale and the Church had a stranglehold monopoly on the product, forgiveness was without doubt the best selling line. If you were a base and sinful type, prone to periodic attacks of the seven deadlies, you were able to pop round to the local 'forgiveness factory' and buy a document called an indulgence which entitled the bearer to freedom from a reprimand in the hereafter for sins that, although confessed, still merited heavenly punishment.

On special offer to robber barons and the like, was a sort of package deal to heaven specially designed for those who by rights should have been heading straight for that other place, where you can't get near the fire for bishops. What you got for your money was a Novem, which was nine days of prayers muttered on your behalf by the vendors after you had shuffled off the old mortal coil. Working on the self-evident principle that you can't take it with you when you go anyway, these were very popular indeed, leaving the professional prayers some pretty tight schedules. The sincerity was a trifle suspect in the eyes of the ordinary man, since it seemed that as soon as one run was over, the monks immediately forgot about that one and began another.

NUMBER OF THE BEAST

Prior to the mid–late 1970s and the totally unhealthy advent of films like 'The Omen' and 'The Exorcist' which seemed to rely on startling effects rather than good scripting and acting, probably not one out of a thousand people would have known the Number of the Beast, the Mark of the Anti-Christ, or whatever you want to call it, to be 666.

Being more pagan than anything else, early Christians read mystic symbolism into almost everything around them, the hot favourite being the numerical value of certain words in Greek or Hebrew notation. Without a shadow of a doubt, the original Number of the Beast was 616 and derived from the reversal of the monogram of Christ which is ☧. When turned around, this becomes ⚡, a figure interpretable as being made up of 'X', | and ⊂; figures representing to the Hebrews the numbers 600, 10 and 6 respectively. Can there be any doubt, they reasoned, that this is the number of Satan?

Well, you can imagine how delighted these early Christians were when it dawned on them that the names of some of their most ardent and efficient persecutors could be made to total 616 in one way or another. Caligula, Nero, Hadrian, Trajan, they all fitted the bill, and all went well until later enemies' names could not be hammered into conformity no matter how they tried. There was nothing for it, a new number had to be found, and find it they did in 666, a number with an altogether better ring to it in that it fell short of the holy number '7' in all aspects.

Titus gave them a bit of trouble because he unsportingly refused to fit any pattern until they decided that his name must be a form of 'Titan', which can be spelt 'Teitan' and, thank heavens, totalled the new number. Looking back, they found that if Nero was referred to as Neron Caesar, then the extra 'n' which was worth fifty points boosted him to the new number as well. Best of all, 'Lateinos', meaning the Roman Empire, added up to 666, so that settled the matter!

The only trouble with playing around with names like this, changing everything that does not suit, is that it can be very much a double-edged sword. If you apply the same tactics to the names of saints, popes and Biblical heroes, you will find dozens that can be made to fit in one way or another. Until the Reformation, the papal crown included the word 'Mysterium' in its inscription which, to everybody's shock and horror, totalled the dreaded number and had to be hurriedly removed.

OSTRACISE
Although this is only applied in the sense of sending someone to Coventry, in the Athens of old it had a much more severe and precise political meaning. Once a year, all the citizens of that city would be called upon to cast votes for anyone that they considered so unpopular or dangerous to the safety of Athens that they should be banished. Any public figure unlucky enough to receive 6,000 such votes was given the order of the boot and told not to come back for ten years.

Each vote was cast on a small piece of shell or tile named 'ostrakon', the word therefore being allied to 'oyster'.

PARADISE

Every religion must have its Paradise, call it Valhalla, Nirvana or Heaven, it does not matter as long as it is there, for that is the pot of gold at the end of the rainbow of self-denial and sacrifice demanded by the rules. The word itself, however, comes from something a little more basic and down to earth, namely the private playgrounds of the old kings of Persia. The 'Pairidaezas' were the royal hunting parks where absolutely anything a chap wanted was there on tap. The Greeks picked up the word in the form of 'paradeisos' and, no doubt ignorant of the sinful, pagan places that the term originally described, the first translators of the Bible into Greek chose the term to stand for the Garden of Eden where, as things turned out, the earthly pleasures of the original paradises were strictly off the menu!

PATTER

Another term that has crossed the floor to sit on the back benches of slang and cant! As stated elsewhere in this section, the clerics of old were forever chuntering away in Latin, leaving a bemused, yet respectful congregation to chip in with the odd 'Amen' or two. Just as anyone who has to repeat something time and time again, on reaching the point in the service when the Paternoster was required, the priests kicked into high gear and rattled it off in an unintelligible manner. The people for whose benefit it was supposedly said took the first part of the word to stand for a fast, smooth line in chat intended to hoodwink.

PERFUME

The original uses of perfumes were considerably less romantic than the current ones in that their main purpose was to mask the repugnant smell of burning flesh and blood at sacrifices. They usually took the form of aromatic gum resins which were burnt along with whatever, or even whoever, so as not to upset the worshippers. Since the term is based on the Latin *per fumum* – 'through smoke' – it is a sister-word of the less glamorous 'fumigate', although the way that some people use the perfumes it can sometimes amount to the same thing.

PITTANCE
An alternative open to monied medievals who did not fancy the idea of coughing up for a nine day wonder (qv) was to leave a bequest for what was known as a pittance. The money was paid annually to the local monks to provide a lash-up banquet in payment for their praying for the donor's salvation on the anniversaries of his death. In the early days, the size of such bequests was quite considerable but, as people wised up a little, they got smaller and smaller until the word took on its current meaning. The ultimate derivation is the Latin *pietas* meaning 'piety'.

PONTIFF
As an alternative term for the Pope, this actually comes from the Latin *pons*, *pontis* – 'a bridge' because, in ancient Rome, the responsibility for the maintenance of the city's bridges lay with the chief priest.

PROPAGANDA
Despite this being the most effective 'passive' political weapon, the word itself is of Roman Catholic origin.

In 1622, the Vatican founded the 'Congregatio de Propaganda Fide' – Council for the Propagation of the Faith – such title soon getting shortened to 'The

Propaganda', for speedy reference. It was the way that the Vatican used to go about convincing others of the error of their misplaced religious conviction that gave the word its dark connotations.

QUAKER
In George Fox's time, slurs like 'Shakers', 'Jerkers', 'Jumpers' and 'Quakers' were always being levelled at 'over the top' religious sects whose members seemed to be incapable of resisting the temptation to twitch about with spiritual fervour during their devotions. Now, if you find yourself the butt of an insult, there's one sure way to take the sting out of its tail, that being to adopt it as a badge of honour. And that's exactly what the Society of Friends did! In fact, Fox took matters a stage further by putting about the story that he himself had given rise to the name by instructing some Derbyshire magistrate to 'quake and tremble at the word of the Lord'. Unfortunately for that story, the alleged incident occurred in 1650 and the term has been located in print in a document dated 1647.

RED LETTER DAYS
In ecclesiastical calendars, all the important feast days and saints' days were marked in red and the others in black.

ROBBING PETER TO PAY PAUL
It is true that in the mid-1500s the proceeds from the estates belonging to St Peter's (Westminster Abbey) were dipped into to fund repairs to St Paul's Cathedral, but this is not the true origin of the saying as is usually put forward. The expression was in common use as early as the 1300s, the names most likely being picked simply because they were common and everyday.

SCAPEGOAT

As part of the Atonement Day rites of the ancient Jews, two goats were brought to the altar. After hearing all the confessions, the priest bestowed the collective sins of the congregation upon one of the animals which was promptly turned out into the wilderness, taking all the evil with it. The other goat was then sacrificed so, unlike the modern counterpart, the scapegoat, or escapegoat, certainly got the better of the deal.

SCARLET WOMAN

St John was responsible for this now thoroughly outdated term for a woman who, whilst perhaps not a full-blown professional girl, could be described as an enthusiastic amateur. In the Bible he claims to have had a vision which included a woman labelled as 'Mother of Harlots' who was arrayed in 'purple and scarlet colour'.

SEVENTH HEAVEN

The Mohammedans, as well as the early English mystical sects, reckoned that there were seven separate heavens to work through, the seventh, and highest, being the home of God, whoever you held him to be.

SHIBBOLETH

Every language has something that everybody else experiences great difficulty with. In English it's 'th' for the French, 'r's' for the Chinese and 'l's' for the Japanese. In Biblical times, it was the word 'shibboleth' for the Ephraimites, that word in Hebrew meaning an ear of corn.

After some battle or another in which the Jews had thrashed the Ephraimites, they took control of all the fords in the Jordan over which the enemy had passed on the way to the battle. All strangers wishing to ford the river had to say 'Shibboleth' if they wanted to live to see old age.

SUB ROSA

The story behind this expression, meaning 'in the strictest confidence', begins in ancient mythology when Venus was caught red-handed giving some vigorous on-the-job training to some deity who had long been the focus of her Ugandan inclinations. It was Harpokrates, the god of silence, who had stumbled across this syzygy, and Venus was making little headway in her quest to convince the interloper that he ought to play the white-god and live up to his title, when along trotted the gross little product of her previous African chats with Mercury, Cupid, the troublesome little toxophilite. Never travelling anywhere without the tools of his dubious trade and a seemingly never-ending supply of red roses, he eventually managed to buy Harpokrates' silence with a rose that never faded and by which he was later always identified. Because of this story, the ceilings of the rooms set aside for diplomatic discussions in the palaces of old, were traditionally decorated with roses as a constant reminder that what was said in such chambers was, quite literally, under the rose.

SUFFRAGETTE AND SUFFRAGE

At the juncture of the tibia and the tarsus in all quadrupeds is a bone that roughly corresponds to the heel bone in humans. To the Romans these were known as 'suffragines' and made ideal little tablets for the casting of votes in elections.

TAWDRY

In Cambridgeshire, there used to be an annual fair held at the Isle of Ely in honour of St Audrey. Traditionally this was a market for some of the finest lace products available but, perhaps inevitably, the affair became debased with cheap trash and a corrupted form of the saint's name came to stand for such.

WALL – GOING TO THE

As far as the common herd were concerned, the churches of yesterday were not the comfortable affairs that they are today. The nobility had seats but that was all. In such times, the finger of heresy or witchcraft was pointed all too easily and not many wished to risk the ramifications of that by not appearing to be a good Christian, or church-goer at any rate. Besides, there was not an awful lot else to do on a typical medieval Sunday. All in all, the churches enjoyed a much higher attendance rate than they do today and, in summer, the press and heat were far too much for the old and the infirm who had to be given places near the walls where it was cooler and they gained additional support, even little seats in the better churches.

THE JUST AND THE
NOT SO JUST

BACKCHAT

Most subcultures have their own jargon, if only to make themselves feel different, but backchat developed for reasons far more practical than things charismatic. Otherwise known as back-slang, this was a code used by petty thieves, barrow-boys and other general undesirables to prevent outsiders, particularly the Old Bill, understanding whatever it was that they were talking about. All words were reversed and sometimes bastardised as well so, if you didn't know the lingo, they might just as well be talking in Russian. 'Police', for example, became 'ecilop', which was cut down to 'slop', which produced the current and rather unpleasant 'The Filth'. The barrow-boys were tagged as 'yobs' because that was the pluralised reversal of 'boy'.

Because the type of person who felt the need for such privacy of public conversation tended not to be the sort of chap you would introduce to your maiden aunt, 'backchat' rapidly became synonymous with rude and abusive talk, and we all know what happened to 'yob'.

BAR – TO BE CALLED TO THE

In days gone by, that which passed for justice was meted out to the multitude in any old building that was large enough to accommodate the proceedings; quite often this meant a barn or some similar building. To separate the officials from the rabble, a rope was strung across and anyone with anything relevant to say was called upon to step up front to the rope and say his piece. Later, when courts became fixed venues in purpose built locations, the now familiar rail replaced the rope and, again, anyone the court wished to hear from was called to step up to the bar to address the bench. When advocacy became a formalised profession the expression simply transferred.

BAWDY

In Shakespeare's day, if you wandered into an inn and asked for bed and board, you might have got something of a surprise, for a 'bawd' was the then term for a working girl. A bawdy-house was a 'nookie factory' – hence our use of 'bawdy' to mean rowdy or a bit 'blue'.

BEYOND THE PALE

This developed in the fourteenth century after an area in Ireland known as the English Pale. Occupying a broad belt down the right-hand side of the country, this described that part of the island which was under the control of the English and people there could expect the protection of the occupying army. Anyone outlawed was evicted from the Pale and had to take his chances in Ireland's answer to the Arizona Badlands. As for the word 'pale', this came from the same source as does 'impale' and 'paling' as in fencing, from the Latin *palus* – a stake – the suggestion being to the boundary.

BLACK MARIA

Every country has a nickname (no pun intended!) for this vehicle; in parts of South America it's called 'mother's heart' because there is always room for one more. The original Black Maria was one Maria Lee, a Negress who was powerfully built and ran a boarding house in the Boston of the late nineteenth century. Her business was just round the corner from the central police station and, not being a lady to put up with any trouble and being possessed of arms like ham shanks, she was not averse to carting trouble-makers round there herself and handing them over to the desk sergeant. Having become something of a local character and had her exploits written up in the local rags, she soon found her name being used for the paddy waggons in Boston, the term later becoming far more widespread.

BLACK SHEEP

There's not much to say about this phrase. Quite simply, this comes from the fact that the wool from black sheep did not command much of a price, so shepherds were not overpleased at the appearance of black lambs and tended to think of them as being unlucky.

BLACKGUARD

Now pronounced 'blaggard' this word is a little passé, to say the least, but its story is worth telling, nevertheless.

The term came to life as a humorously bestowed title applied to the lowest of the low who spent their lives in the kitchens of sixteenth-century castles tending the fires, cleaning out the grates and scrubbing the pots. These, it must be remembered, were the days before hygiene had been invented, so members of the Black Guard would not have been the cleanest members of the household.

Such mock military titles are still common today, members of various trades or professions getting called the 'Whatever Brigade' or navvies labelled the 'Queen's Own Pick and Shovel' or 'McAlpine's Fusiliers'. Anyway, the term 'blackguard' fell into disrepute because of the atrocious wages that they were, or more often weren't, paid. You see, if they wanted any of the creature comforts, they had to go moonlighting as muggers and footpads to pick up the wherewithal, and most people were of the no doubt well-founded belief that a blackguard would probably do someone in for a couple of groats.

BLACKMAIL

Although most blackmail demands do come through the post, the 'mail' part of the word has nothing to do with the GPO. The term is a hangover from Old English where it described the protection money extracted from the landowners along the Scottish border by the local

Mafia. Prior to this, the first formal meaning of 'blackmail' was a rent paid to a landlord in corn, labour or coinage other than silver; 'mail' on its own having a meaning of tax or rent. Higher rents that required payment in silver were known as 'whitemails'. 'Blackmail' probably transferred to the activities of the border racketeers because they often took payment in the form of supplies and food.

BLOW AWAY – TO

Perhaps it is inevitable in a country where, for example, New York alone has more murders in a week (58 is the record so far!) than some countries experience in a year, that the Americans are going to have a wealth of expressions synonymous with killing someone. This one, which crept into English through the back door opened by the recent glut of imported American 'chewing gum for the eyes', started out in the local black slang of New Orleans as a result of the weird jazz funerals for which that city is famous. En route to the grave, a band, mainly made up of brass instruments, plays the coffin through the streets in a process known locally as 'blowing someone away'.

BOOTLEGGER

During the American Prohibition this was the nickname for the delivery boys who carried large, flat bottles to the private punter inside their tall boots.

BUSHWACKER

Forgetting all the tired old jokes about perpetrating GBH on the shrubbery, bacon trees and ham bushes and so forth, this Americanism stems from the Dutch *bosch wachter* which meant forest keeper, or a sort of bush ranger/fire warden. The spelling altered to 'wacker' and took on its unpleasant meaning after the term had become the recognised label for men hired to go off in a gang and clear tracts of land of trees and shrubbery – whacking the bushes with their axes, or whatever. It was mainly saddle-tramps and drifters who signed on for such work and it was not exactly unknown for them to ambush and kill travellers who were unfortunate enough to cross their path, robbery being the motive.

CAT – TO LET THE CAT OUT OF THE BAG

It was the same bit of sharp practice of old that gave rise to this as produced 'buying a pig in a poke' and getting 'sold a pup'.

Fairgrounds and carnivals have long been favourite locations for sharks to get their teeth into Joe Public's wallet, this never being truer than in medieval times when an old trick was the selling of sucking pigs that weren't! The dupe would be shown a real live piglet in a sack which was promptly tied up again and put down while the price was haggled over. When the deal was struck, the mark was given a different sack that actually contained a muted cat and a bit of ballast, or a puppy. If the victim opened the sack before leaving the vendor, then the cat would literally be out of the bag and the game up. 'Poke', the diminutive of which is pocket', was quite a common word for a small sack.

CHICANERY

Trickery of the legal variety that takes its name from the Persian for an early form of crooked polo stick. This word, *chuagan* moved into French where it became *chicane* and got applied to a rather butch version of hockey-cum-polo that was played on foot with a kind of 'if you can't hit the ball hit the bloke who's got it' mentality. The game was extremely popular in Languedoc where it was played with so much skullduggery that the term began to assume its current meaning.

CLINK – IN
Just one of the numerous slang terms for prison. Until it was destroyed during the Gordon Riots, there was a well-known prison called Clink Prison which was located in Southwark.

COUP DE GRACE
Back in the good old bad old days, confessions weren't half the bother to obtain that they are today. If you wanted someone to own up to a particular crime or act, you simply took him down to the dungeons and started breaking bits off him until he saw the light and signed anything that was put in front of him. Since one good turn deserves another, it was considered good form to put the poor chap out of his misery as soon as you had got what you wanted, that killing blow being called the 'coup de grâce' or 'the mercy blow'.

CULPRIT
In medieval courts, the Clerk of the Court, having read out the charges and heard the defendant plead, would address the bench as follows: '*Culpable, prest d'averrer nostre bille*', this meaning 'He is guilty and I am ready to prove our (the people's) case'. In trial records this was usually shortened to *cul. prit*, the second word being an alternative form of *prest*. Incredibly conservative and traditionist as the legal profession is, it was a long time before the word was allowed in court to describe the defendants themselves, the first man ever being so addressed being the Earl of Pembroke when on trial for murder in 1678.

DEAD RINGER

Used to describe someone or something of identical appearance to the original, this epithet comes from the colourful world of horse-racing, or horse-race fiddling, to be more precise.

In the times before mass communication ruined many a good fiddle, it was far from uncommon for a red-hot runner to be doctored up to look like a well-known nag so that a packet could be made on the long odds that the bookies would post on that entrant. The ruse worked just as well in reverse, except the money was put on the horse that everyone thought should come in second. The bogus entry was called a ringer because all concerned had to be involved in a ring-deal; the owner, the jockey, the trainer, etc.

DEED POLL

Contracts between two parties used to be made on what was called 'deed indenture', because the agreement was drawn up in counterpart on the one piece of parchment which was then cut or ripped apart in irregular fashion to prevent later forgeries which, of course, would not marry up when twinned. The scalloped edges seen on many a legal document are a reminder of the old practice. Deed poll, on the other hand, denotes an agreement, such as changing one's name, that is entered into by just one party, with no obligation or commitment required of a second person, the contract therefore being drawn up on straight-edged, or polled, paper.

FAKE

Firmly based on the German *fegen*, which meant to refurbish or clean up, this term first made an appearance in English in the opening decades of the nineteenth century with the spelling 'feague'. The word first emerged in horse-trader's cant to describe the process of tarting up an animal for sale by employing tricks that disguised the animal's true age. The favourite trick of these erstwhile used-car salesmen was to turn a horse's speedo back by cleaning up and reshaping its teeth, a process known as bishoping due to the mitre-like shape of the teeth after faking.

FAST AND LOOSE

Yet another contribution to English from the fairground rip-off artists of yesterday! Just like 'find the lady' nobody won at 'fast and loose' which was played, not with cards, but with a leather strap and a metal skewer. The strap was doubled over to produce a loop at the middle when rolled up and held fast. The punter was given a skewer, and when the shyster cried 'Loose!', he allowed the strap to unwind under its own steam and the sucker had to stop it in its tracks by arresting the loop with a single stab of his skewer. Try it sometime. It's impossible!

FILTHY LUCRE

Despite the relatively modern ring to this expression, it does in fact come from the Bible; I Timothy 3: 2–3, to be exact. Under discussion in the text are the qualities demanded of anyone wishing to become a bishop; drunkenness, fighting and being 'greedy of filthy lucre' are just three of the idiosyncrasies that are considered absolute noes in prospective candidates. 'Filthy', in this context, means dishonestly obtained – backhanders and the like. Actually, the Bible is responsible for bringing the term 'lucre' into disrepute; it is a perfectly respectable word now thought to be slang, or not quite proper. 'Lucrative', on the other hand, enjoys quiet respectability as a synonym for 'profitable'.

GAZUMPING

It was the mid–late seventies before this stolen Yiddish-ism passed into everyday language due to the rapid escalation of fiddling on the house market. Before it made its debut in English it had been fairly widely used in the American motor trade to describe pretty much the same tactics. It is based on the Yiddish term for a swindle – *gezumph*.

GOON

E. C. Segar's monumentally successful 'Popeye' cartoon strip was responsible for pushing this word into the general swim. In 1935, he introduced a new character to the strip – Alice the Goon, who was a large yet incredibly stupid creature with an unerring ability to bump into and break almost everything that she came into proximity with. Segar certainly didn't coin the word, for it had been around for some time by then, serving as a term for a strike-breaker, amongst other things.

It was thanks to the fact that 95 per cent of GIs were hand-reared on chewing gum, cartoons and momma's apple pie that the public got their hands on the term. In the Second World War POW camps, American service-men called their German guards 'goons' and, in a fairly logical step, the word moved into civilian parlance with connotations of heavy-handedness and thuggery.

HOOK OR BY CROOK – BY

Meaning 'by whatever means', this dates from the Middle Ages when tenants had the right to collect fire-wood from their landlord's estate. This does not mean that the peasants were allowed to swarm over the place wielding axes, their rights being restricted to the gathering of fallen wood or that which could be pulled down low with a shepherd's crook and be hacked off with a bill-hook.

HOOLIGAN

Wherever the Irish have accumulated in any numbers they have soon managed to establish a fine reputation for drunkenness and brawling, nineteenth-century London being no exception. One family in particular, the Hooligans of Southwark, attracted the attention of the London press with monotonous regularity, having raised thuggery and petty crime to the level of a science.

Funnily enough, because of the then solid relationship between the British and Russian courts, the term was picked up by visiting Russians and is still alive and well in that language today.

IGNORAMUS

This took on its current meaning from its use in that sense by frustrated prosecution lawyers who had had their indictments thrown out by sixteenth-century Grand Juries. If that body considered the indictment insufficiently well founded to proceed for trial, they returned the document with the word 'Ignoramus' written on the back. Holding, in legal circles, a meaning of 'We take no notice of it', this was taken as an indication of the jury's stupidity by the prosecuting council who was peeved about his case's rejection.

KANGAROO COURT

With the acquisition of Australia as a new colony, the whisper went through the courts that anyone they could possibly deport would be very gratefully received. Anxious to oblige, most judges simply couldn't be bothered to spend much time establishing the facts of a case brought against a commoner for some trivial crime because, whether he privately thought the defendant to be innocent or not, the judge felt it his patriotic duty to fill the next shipment for Botany Bay. After a short while, the commoners realised exactly what was happening and coined the above expression.

KIBOSH

Before informing someone that he is about to get a 'suspended' sentence the judges of most countries used to don a black hat or simply a square of black material, and Ireland was no exception. In that country the item was called the *cie bais*, the second word being pronounced 'bosh'.

LYNCH LAW

It does seem more than a little ghoulish that the Americans and the Irish should squabble with each other in an effort to claim the dubious eponymous honour of having given this word to the English language. Each nation puts forward various eighteenth- and nineteenth-century characters named Lynch who, during troubled and lawless eras, set up unofficial courts and festooned the local orchards with 'strange fruit'. Nor is this hot-blooded predilection for DIY justice restricted to our colonial cousins for, as recently as 27 October 1958, a gang of public-spirited Londoners dispatched a suspected murderer with the unlikely name of Panglam Godolan.

The main trouble with the bulk of these apocryphal-sounding stories is that when the word 'lynch' first emerged it was not written with a capital 'L', nor did it mean to execute; it meant to tar and feather, to bullwhip someone, or just generally rough them up. Of long service in English is the word 'linch', meaning to beat or handle a person roughly. The ultimate point of origin is most likely the sixteenth-century 'linch-pin', an item of ship's equipment better known today as a belaying pin, these being favourite conversational aids employed by drunken sailors engaged in intellectual debate with a fellow bilge-rat who was failing to appreciate the salient points of the argument.

MAN OF STRAW
There is one theory that maintains this expression derives from the law courts of London of the eighteenth century, where men prepared to go into the witness box and swear to anything for a price used to hang around outside and indicate their availability for hire by keeping a wisp of straw in their mouths.

MARK OF CAIN
Since Cain is best remembered for killing his brother, people use this expression in completely the wrong context; they apply it to those whom they think have the look of a murderer. The trouble with this is that the Bible does not say that the 'mark' was put on Cain to brand him as a murderer, but to protect him from those who felt disposed to kill him for his crime.

MORGUE
This term has travelled a rather peculiar path that starts in the jargon of the prison officers of the late nineteenth-century French penal system. In French, *morgue* holds a prime meaning of arrogance and big-headedness. Because of this, it was used by wardens to describe that part of a maximum security prison set aside as an induction centre where new inmates were scrutinised in an attempt to weed out hard-nuts and the 'you'll never break me'

types before they were allocated cells in the main body of the prison, where it was feared that, if they were admitted with an unbroken air, they could become hero figures, attract a following and become potentially very dangerous.

Next, the word made a massive lateral jump when it became the nickname of the building set up by the Paris authorities for the purpose of putting on display all the bodies that were found floating in the river or lying about making the streets untidy. Anyone with a missing friend or relative regarded the place as the first port of call where they could cast an eye over the latest batch of cadavers. It was this sense of looking or watching that caused the transfer, and 'morgue' later ceased to be regarded as a slang term and was granted the mantle of respectability.

NARK

A tag for an informant which was more popular at the turn of the century than it is today, when members of that dangerous tight-rope-walking club prefer to be known as grasses, preferably super-grasses because then they get much more money and a new face. If their chums get to them first, the nark doesn't get any money, he just gets the new face! 'Nark' is based on *nak*, the Romany for nose; the connection between noses and information continuing through 'snitch' and 'snout'.

OLD BILL – THE

Around the time of the First World War, a cartoonist with the peculiar name of Charles Bruce Bairnsfather was all the rage. When the conflict started in earnest, Bairnsfather started a series entitled 'Fragments from France' which always featured two soldiers, one of whom was Bairnsfather's most famous creation, Old

Bill. Due to the character's popularity, the authorities made use of him on posters with pertinent messages regarding collective war-effort – shoulders to the wheel, home economy and all of the usual stuff. Perhaps to give extra weight to the points raised, Old Bill was put into the uniform of a special constable, which caused his name to transfer to London's finest.

ON THE SPOT

It is said that the pirates of old operated under a sort of code of practice which, when reduced to basics, demanded that members of the so-called Brotherhood nicked everything that wasn't nailed down, killed all men who crossed them at sea and raped all the women, so, unless one of them flipped out and confused these last two it is difficult to imagine just what depths of depravity rendered ·a member unacceptable to his fellows. Nevertheless, traitors and violators of the code were always served notice that their end was in sight by being presented with a piece of paper marked with a plain black spot. This was supposed to be reminiscent of the ace of spades, a card that is almost universally regarded as the death-card.

PHONEY

Perhaps influenced by the Yiddish *pfui*, which also produced 'phooey', or by the Irish *fainne*, meaning a ring, this term first cropped up in the States around the end of the last century, when it was used by con-men as a name for the artificial diamond ring that they used in one of the oldest switch-tricks of all. At that time, the spelling was definitely 'fawney' but, most likely in an attempt to make the word respectable, it was given the 'ph' spelling almost as soon as it had landed in England. This had the effect of hinting at classical origins that were nevertheless foney!

PLAYING BOTH ENDS AGAINST THE MIDDLE

This is a donation from the poker tables of the American West where cheating quite often had terminal results. A deck of cards in skilful, if not wholly honest hands, can be a fascinating thing to watch and a proficient cheat is hellishly difficult to catch out, especially if he is playing both ends against the middle. This entails the deal alternating between the top and the bottom of the deck, hence the expression 'dealing someone off the bottom of the deck'.

PRIVATE EYE

When the now famous Pinkerton Detective Agency first set up shop, all the company paperwork had the company motif of a vigilant-looking human eye printed on it. Some spoil-sports say that this is not the true origin which is, they say, nothing more interesting than a play on private 'i', as in investigator.

QUACK

We have the Dutch to thank for this lovely term for a bogus doctor. It is nothing more than a shortened version of *kwaksalver*, which was their name for the charlatans who worked the road, stopping at every hamlet to quack to the locals about his salves or medicines.

QUIBBLE

Only government departments can match lawyers when it comes to the fine art of gobbledegook, and it was the overuse of the Latin *quibus* – 'to whom' – in legal documentation that gave rise to this term for petty-fogging and pernickety argument.

RACKET

If you saw the film 'The Sting', then you will have seen a sophisticated version of the con-game that put this term into the public's mouth. It is called 'gragracket'. The finer points of the game alter all the time, but the principle remains blissfully the same. The con-men set up a bogus operation, such as a betting shop or a casino, both of which tend to have large sums of money lying around. Once a few plump victims have been drawn in and have been made at ease, a right royal rumpus is caused (phoney police raids were usually the favourite) and, whilst their attention is distracted, someone grabs all their money amidst the racket.

RINGLEADER

Originally this applied to the leader of a coven of witches. Most of their ceremonies involved what was called a ring-dance which was led by the head witch, who was quite often referred to as the ringleader.

SCREW

As applied to a prison officer, this dates back to the days when most locks were comparatively simple devices that worked on a worm-drive principle. As for its service as a slang term for wages, this arose in the days before wage packets when the pay was issued screwed up in pieces of paper with the man's name written on it for identification.

SHORT SHRIFT

'Shrift' is derived from the Anglo-Saxon *scrifan*, meaning to receive a confession. Short shrift occurred when a hangman was on a tight schedule or thought that the condemned man had been so active that if given time on the gallows to reel off all of his sins, he would die of old age rather than the rope. Although it started out describing hurried executions, it soon found a place in general speech to describe the treating of someone in a summary manner.

SPIV

Gradually fading from popular usage, this earlier term for a fly-boy arose as part of police jargon and seems to be an acronym of 'suspect persons and itinerant vendors'.

SPREE

Invariably paired with 'drunken' or 'spending' this word's unruly overtones are ever present because the term is derived from the Gaelic *spreath*, which meant 'stolen cattle'. The original sprees were raiding parties into someone's territory.

STIR – IN

There are three strong possibilities regarding the origin of this, so it's a case of take your pick. Number one is the Gypsy *stirpen* which means 'prison' and is therefore a likely contender. Number two is the Old English *styr*, meaning a penalty, and, last but by no means least, comes the 'porridge principle' which maintains that since that revolting breakfast food used to be known as 'stirabout' and constituted the prisoner's basic food, it must be the true origin. It could well be, after all, that 'doing porridge' is synonymous with 'in stir'.

SYCOPHANT

Back in the very early days of Athens, it was considered a serious offence to export or otherwise traffic in figs since they were thought to be sacred. With the passage of time and the realisation that figs moved just about everything but the spirit, the law effectively lapsed to become one of those legal curiosities that every civilisation has sitting in its statute books. In reality, no one gave a damn about the 'illegal' fig trade; in fact, it was lining quite a few pockets, and the last thing that the authorities wanted was to be informed by some obsequious creep about what they already knew, thus being put in a position of having to act and implement outdated legislation. The Greeks coined the word *sycophantein* to describe such grovellers trying to ingratiate themselves with the powers that be, building that term on the foundation of *sykon* – a fig – and *phainein*, which meant 'to show'.

THIRD DEGREE

The Masons don't give much away but they have given us this phrase, usually reserved for police interrogations of such intensity that the subject gets so overwrought that he mounts a vicious attack on his tormentors, repeatedly striking them on the knee-caps with his groin and butting the truncheons hidden in their pockets.

The highest order attainable in the funny-handshake club is that of Master Mason, otherwise known as The Third Degree. Those aspiring to such dizzy heights are subjected to some pretty gruelling tests and interviews in an attempt to gauge their suitability.

THUG

Although in general usage this denotes suborders like the Millwall Missing Links *et al.*, 'thug', alternatively spelt 'thag', does have a quite specific application to any member of a now long dead brotherhood of professional assassins who operated in India, until their eradication by Lord William Bentinck in a campaign lasting from 1828 through to 1835.

Basing their self-anointed name on the Sanskrit *sthaga*, which meant to cheat or swindle, the Thugs worshipped the goddess of destruction, Kali, their belief being that the more people they bumped off in this world, the nicer she'd be to them in the next. To count in their total, a kill had to be performed to a strict set of rules and rites, and death had to be effected by strangulation – preferably with a prayer scarf with a rupee knotted in one corner. They survived on the money stolen from their victims.

TICH OR TITCHY

For such a small word with such a small meaning, there is quite a long and tall story that goes with it!

The tale begins on 20 April 1854, when Sir Roger Tichborne, the heir to the Tichborne estates and fortunes, embarked on a ship bound for Jamaica out of Rio, never to be seen again, the vessel having done a disappearing act. Sir Roger's mother stoically refused to accept the fact of her son's death and immediately mounted a protracted campaign offering rewards around the globe for information as to the whereabouts of her son. Needless to say, apart from a few false sightings prompted by the hope of reward rather than actuality, she was wasting her time.

In 1866, by which time Lady Tichborne was well and truly gaga, there emerged from Australia a singularly repugnant con-man who was to become known as the Tichborne Claimant. Among the innumerable glaring differences between the lost son and the uncultivated, tattooed slob who had turned up, was physical appearance. Roger had disappeared weighing an elegant 9 stone and Arthur Orton, as his name turned out to be, tipped the scales at 24 stone. None of this mattered to

101

the senile old girl who welcomed Orton with open cheque books and took him into her home. He milked her for everything he could get until her death, after which the family found him alternative accommodation, guaranteed rent-free for the next fourteen years.

Born at the same time as all this, was one Harry Ralph who went on to become one of the most successful music hall comedians. A dwarf, he had at birth been not only extremely small, but also extremely fat, which caused his parents to give him the nickname 'Tichborne'. In the altered form of 'Tich' or 'Little Tich', Ralph used this as a stage name which produced the currently used term.

WELSH ON A DEBT

Throughout history, various races have become the target of the worst kind of British humour. When it was the Dutch, we had 'Dutch courage', 'Dutch treat' and 'Dutch Uncle'; when it was the French we had 'French leave', and 'French disease', and currently it's the Irish. In the distant past the Welsh were not exactly the greatest anglophiles around and we were not over-enamoured of them either. When Englishmen found themselves in debt up to their necks with the debtors prison just around the corner, most of them did a runner across the Welsh border to escape their creditors, who, having more to lose than the debtor, were unwilling to risk their lives by going after him.

WEST – TO HAVE GONE

From about the close of the twelfth century until 1759, the infamous Tyburn gibbet was a permanent fixture near what is now the junction of Edgware Road and Bayswater Road, just across from Marble Arch. Such a location would have put it to the west of what was then the city of London and this expression developed in thieves' cant to describe a chum who had gone for a spin in the municipal tumbril.

FOOD AND FASHION

ANTIMACASSAR

These survive purely for reasons of decoration, whereas back in the late 1800s when they first put in an appearance, they served a very practical purpose. The dandies had taken to plastering their hair with perfumed oil which meant that they left heavy deposits of 20/50s on every chair they sat in. The answer to this problem was forthcoming in the form of what is now called an antimacassar, so called because the most popular hair-oil was brand-named 'Macassar', and was imported from Mangkasara in the Celebes Isles.

BAKER'S DOZEN

There's nothing new in the cheating-about-eating game. Not having any monosodium glutamate in the old days didn't stop the adulteration of food. The millers were fiddling the bakers by adding plaster of Paris to the flour to eke it out and make it look purer than it really was, and the bakers were always adding alum to the bread to make it look nice and white. It must have been like taking a bite out of a brick! Apart from all these little tricks, the weight of loaves was always being trimmed that little bit to boost the profit. In an attempt to reduce the notorious and wholesale fiddling in the baking trade, fifteenth-century England introduced a strict system of weights and measures, the penalties for infringement thereof being severe. When delivering orders, bakers took to throwing in an extra loaf per dozen, this being known as the vantage loaf. The reason for this was simple; it is extremely difficult to guarantee the cooked weight of an item such as bread, and it was thought safer to give a loaf away rather than to risk the chance of a heavy fine.

BALDERDASH

Hardly a piece of modern slang, but it does still hang around the fringes of current usage. Originally the word meant a totally incongruous mixture of booze, gin and sherry, for example. The term transferred due to the notion that if you drank balderdash you would end up talking it as well.

BARMY

It is true that there used to be a famous lunatic asylum at Barming Heath, just outside Maidstone, but, despite numerous attempts to link the two, the word 'barmy', with all its association with lunacy was around long before the institution. It comes from the brewing trade where the froth and scum that collects on the surface of fermenting malt liquor is known as barm. It periodically needs to be collected and the less fastidious workers were not above working on a 'waste not want not' principle which was guaranteed to blow them out of their skulls.

BEANO

A popular term for a knees-up that still appears in its full and proper form of 'beanfeast'.

There are two likely possibilities as to the origin of the saying, the first being the revels of Twelfth Night when a cake in which a bean had been hidden was divided amongst all present, and the one who got the bean became a sort of 'king for a day'. The other idea is that it comes from the annual feast given by a feudal lord for his underlings, the traditional fare being a beangoose – so named from a bean-shaped mark on its bill.

BEEFEATERS

There are probably as many pseudo-historical stories, each complete with 'authenticated' quotes, etc., as there are members of this very old regiment. There is no connection between the dreamt-up term of 'buffetier', or from the groundless idea that they ate nothing but beef. The origin is quite straightforwardly 'beef eater', an old derogatory slur for a well-fed menial in a noble household; less fortunate servants got called 'loaf eaters'. There was quite a bit of prestige in belonging to the regiment since they got to perform some personal service to the royal household, standing round and looking impressive at state functions and that sort of thing. Because of this status, other regiments suffering from an attack of the jealousies gave them the nickname which was later adopted as a regimental badge of honour.

BEST BIB AND TUCKER

In the seventeenth century, dining was not always the genteel affair that, by comparison, it can be today; people sometimes used to eat like horses – quite literally. Because the heavy, padded clothing was virtually impossible to wash, not that they bothered much anyway, bibs were commonplace and very dressy. The even more ornate counterpart for women was called a tucker, which gave rise to expressions like 'tuck in' and 'tuck shop'. The bib was named from the Latin *bibere* – to drink – the man being considered more likely to slop his ale down his doublet than a woman, and the tucker from 'tuck' which was an early variant of 'tug', an allusion to the usual method of removal.

BEVY

This has two basic meanings in English, firstly as a rather patronising collective noun for women, and secondly as a slang term for the amber fluid. Both, funnily enough, derive from the Latin *bibere* which means to drink, and which in later Italian became *beva*. No explanation is needed for 'bevy's' application to beer, but its use in connection with women is quite interesting. It was first used to describe groups of animals that were timid and who, as a result, banded together to drink so that the safeguard of vigilance was there by virtue of numbers. Because women were once regarded as timid creatures (surely some mistake!) they picked up the tag as a collective noun.

BLACKJACK

Life as a barmaid has not changed much over the centuries; there will always be those customers who presume that 'if she's working in a pub, she must be on the game' and that they are perfectly entitled to a sweaty-fingered fumble every time that the poor girl gets within groping range. The early tavern maids, however, did have one good defence – their blackjacks! These were thick, heavy leather jugs that had been stiffened on the outside with tar and, if someone really stepped out of line as they moved about the tavern serving ale, these erstwhile Bet Lynches were known to issue instant hangovers with them. Before long, 'blackjack' was a widely accepted form for a club or cosh.

BLOOMERS

Just as today's hardline feminist seems to be struggling for a personal identity amidst a sea of uniformed anonymity, their counterparts in the America of the mid-1800s also used dress as a banner.

Prominent in the American Women's Rights Movement was one Elizabeth Smith-Miller whose main hobby-horse was dress reform. In an ill-advised move

110

towards what she called 'rational dress for women', she came up with a hoot of a get-up that consisted of loose, Turkish-style trousers that were gathered at the ankle, a short, hooped skirt that went over the top of the trousers, a closely tailored monkey-jacket and a very broad-brimmed hat. The overall impression was not unlike a double-decker mushroom. Smith-Miller would appear to have had sufficient sense not to sport her own disaster to the same extent as did one of her contemporaries, Amelia Jenks Bloomer, who wore said attire everywhere that she went to lecture for the movement.

Unfortunately, the women of America were not quite ready for such revolutionary fashion, and the country voiced its considered opinion in such a way that Bloomer soon divested herself of her bloomers. She spent the rest of her life trying to do likewise with the erroneously bestowed accolade of having designed the fiasco herself and the dubious honour of having her name synonymous with loose-fitting knickers.

BLUE STOCKING

Derisively applied to a woman who forsakes all else in favour of intellectual pursuits and tends to be a crashing bore about it, this entered English thanks to a lady named Elizabeth Montague. Distressed by what she considered society's unhealthy preoccupation with having a good time, she organised the suitable antidote in the form of learned gatherings where the meaning of life could be discussed over tea and crumpets. In an effort to align her meetings with the heady informality of similar Paris gatherings, Montague passed the word around that the gentlemen need not consider the wearing of the traditionally formal black stockings to be necessary. One of the more prominent members, a Mr Benjamin Stillingfleet, habitually posed around in blue stockings, alluding to the Paris-based Bas Bleu Club which had been a famous club for French 'heavies' in the seventeenth century. Next thing, Montague herself started wearing blue stockings which caused such a stir that the term has long survived her.

BOWLER HAT

Despite this hat's indissoluble links with the City, it actually started life as a country riding hat. It was a Norfolk landowner named William Coke who, fed up with the way his traditional tall riding hat was knocked off by low branches and the wind, designed what is now called the bowler some time around 1850. He took his design to Locks of St James and asked them to make him a few. They turned the job over to a manufacturer named Beaulieu who saw the potential and went into production. Rather like Decca records turning the Beatles out on to the street, Locks were less than chuffed at having farmed out what they thought was just some deranged bumpkin's flight of fancy, and, to this day, prefer people within their ear-shot to call 'that hat' a coke or a hard felt.

Actually, it's worth mentioning that when the bowler's predecessor, the topper, first hit the streets, there was all hell to pay. In 1797, James Hetherington, dare-devil and young blade about town, stepped into the London air (and history) wearing the very first top hat. Now it must be remembered that these were the days before palates had been jaded by television and he did cause a minor riot. Women started fainting in the crowd that he had accumulated about him and, when a child ended up with a broken arm after getting jostled under a carriage, Hetherington was arrested. Charged with causing a breach of the peace for having 'appeared on the public highway wearing upon his head a tall structure of shining lustre and calculated to disturb those of a timid disposition', he was bound over to keep the peace in penalty of £50.

CAROUSE

This is an odd word and it derives from the German *gar aus* which means 'completely empty', especially in relation to a beer stein. It also served as a somewhat pointed shout for more ale in the German taverns of old, so, too many 'Gar aus!' and a man was likely to carouse.

CHOW

An Americanism that crept into the English language due to the presence of vast numbers of Chinese coolies working on the railroad projects in the West. It comes from a kind of 'Chinglish' that arose, it being based on the Mandarin *ch'ao* which means to cook or to fry.

COASTERS

Today these are nothing more than little mats for glasses and decanters, but in times gone by they did coast up and down the long banqueting tables laden with food. If you have ever tried holding a platter containing a goose, or whatever, at arms length to pass it to another diner, then you would know why they used to have little carts on the table so that people could push things up and down to each other.

COCK A HOOP

When it became time to crack the odd barrel or two at the village fete, the stop-cocks were knocked out of the air-bleeds and left on one of the metal hoops around the barrel so that the beer could flow more freely and everyone could get well and truly 'cock a hooped'.

COCKTAIL

Most of the stories attached to the origin of this word are just as colourful and difficult to swallow as are the obnoxious concoctions themselves. For what it is worth, the following are the more believable of the probabilities.

It is perhaps the Americans who lay the strongest claim to the parenthood of this word; there is certainly more of a cocktail cult over there than here where 99 per cent of drinkers consider these five-star fruit salads to be nothing more than a prissy affectation. That the drinks themselves first raised their ugly heads in the States seems to be beyond dispute, they being first defined in 1806 in an American publication entitled, *Balance and Colombian Repository*. It is far from impossible that the term arose as a result of an analogy between the different colours in a fighting-cock's tail and the different constituents of the drinks; perhaps even the peacock was in mind. In the South they get much more specific by nominating New Orleans restaurateur Antoine Peychaud who, it is claimed, first mixed such drinks and served them in tiny glasses known as *coquetiers*, the French for egg-cups.

France herself puts forward the perfectly reasonable suggestion that the origin lies in the name of a mixed drink from the Gironde that was called *coquetel*, this brew being all the rage with the good citizens of Paris as they slaved away over a hot guillotine. It was *coquetel*, the French maintain, that emerged in the French quarters of New Orleans and influenced M. Peychaud's contributions to the great American hangover.

The only plausible domestic claim comes, understandably enough, from the cock-fighting circles of yesteryear. In what sounds like an ill-advised move towards keeping their birds in fighting trim, the owners used to feed them a vile brew that consisted of ale, gin, herbs, bread and flour. This electric soup was even taken as a tonic by the cock-fighting fraternity themselves, which could well explain why the cockpits of old tended to get a trifle out of hand from time to time. Cock-bread-ale, as this mixture was known, later shortened its name to 'cockale' and subsequently formed the foundations for 'cocktail'.

COLD SHOULDER – TO GIVE SOMEONE THE

One of the rules of chivalry dictated that no knight could refuse another hospitality and stabling facilities for as long as he required them. Now, this was all well and good provided that the visitor played fair and did not take advantage, but, then as now, there were always those who just couldn't tell when the party was over. The broadest possible hint that the reluctant host could drop, short of attacking the parasite, was to present him with cold shoulder of mutton for a meal one night – food normally reserved for servants and the like.

CORDON BLEU

As an indication of a level of attainment, this is absolutely useless because there is no issuing body; anyone can bestow or lay claim to such a title, and those that really are good don't need the accolade. Not surprisingly, the term originated in France.

In their heyday, the Knights Grand Cross of the Holy Ghost were not known for stinting themselves when it came to their frequent banquets, in fact they were the talk of the town. As with our own Knights of the Garter, the members of the order were immediately recognisable by their distinctive pale blue neck-ribbons and *un repas de cordon bleu* soon became a jocular designation for a meal that someone reckoned was good enough to set before the aforementioned knights. This usage – reinforced by the fact that it was not unknown at the real banquets for any chef who had outdone himself to be called to the hall and presented with a strip of blue ribbon by the diners – gradually caused the expression to become the nebulous, ill-defined thing that it is today.

DESSERT
This derives from the French *desservir*, which means to clear away the dishes. Such an apparently illogical name was chosen because the dessert cannot be served until the plates, dishes and general clutter of the main course has been cleared away.

DRESSED TO THE NINES
There is no particular significance to the number nine here because the last word of the expression is in fact a corruption of the Middle English *eyne*. Originally appearing as 'dressed to then eynes' – dressed to the eyes – it slowly altered as time worked its 'send three and fourpence' magic. Exactly the same thing happened to 'donkey's years', which used to be 'donkey's ears'.

EAT HUMBLE PIE
Probably through deliberate steps, the middle word was altered from 'umble' to 'humble', because of the very meaning of the phrase. Ultimately derived from the Latin *lumulus* – a loin – 'umbles' used to refer to the offal of a deer which was used to make a pie for the huntsmen while the lord and his chums scoffed the venison.

EPICUREANISM
There is a widely held yet totally groundless belief that Epicurus advocated the blind, headlong pursuit of pleasures of the flesh and the dining table, which led to his name becoming synonymous with gluttony. Actually, what the man was trying to get across at the turn of the second century BC was that pleasure should be regarded as a natural and perfectly healthy objective of everyone, but a carefully balanced pleasure arising from a life of moderation in all things. The trouble was that at the time

Epicurus was mooting this rather innocuous 'philosophy', the whole of Athens was heavily into mental masochism, everybody who was anybody was practising self-denial and the teachings of the Stoics and the Cynics were all the rage. Diogenes, 'The Dog', to those of sufficiently strong stomachs to get near enough to the man to hear what he had to say (which is why his followers were labelled Cynics, from the Greek *kynikos* – dog-like), was reckoned to roll over in his barrel at the very mention of the word 'pleasure'.

FAIR ISLE KNITTING PATTERNS

The current form is attributable to, of all things, Moorish culture from the shores of northern Africa.

After Drake and his Plymouth Hoe Crown Green Association had well and truly put paid to any hope of a no-claims bonus on the Spanish Armada, Medina Sidonia & Co., cut off from a direct route home, beat a hasty retreat up the left-hand side of England with the intention of shaking off their pursuers, and dodged round the top of Ireland to sneak home that way. Many never made it. They were driven progressively further and further north until several ships foundered on the rocks off the Orkney and Shetland Isles. The happy, friendly islanders couldn't believe their luck at this windfall whom they merrily slaughtered and stripped of everything they possessed – the wrecked ships as well. On Fair Isle, this had the effect of bringing the locals into contact with the rich and intricate Moorish patterns and designs on their booty, which the women promptly built into the island's knitting tradition, there even being one design named The Armada Cross.

FEDORA

In 1882, Sardou, the French dramatist, wrote a play expressly for Sarah Bernhardt. The type of hat that is now known as a fedora was worn in the production of the same name – 'Fédora'.

FILLET

Reserved for the more delicate and therefore expensive cuts of meat, this is actually based on the French word for string, *filet*, since it usually applies to cuts that are boned, rolled, and tied up with string before cooking.

GARNISH

This word has not so much made a lateral jump as flung itself bodily from one side of the language to the other and landed in the kitchen. In early French *garnesche* meant to warn a town or castle of impending attack. Naturally enough, the occupants wouldn't just thank the bringer of such tidings and then go back to sleep again, they would immediately start dashing around and, by the time the enemy turned up, everything was ready for them in that the battlements would be bristling, or 'garnished', with all the paraphernalia of medieval defence.

It was with this military application that the term first entered our native tongue, but later, when the English nobility became trendy, got bored with roast beef and venison and went all continental in the scullery, the word shot across to describe the embellishments on the new cooking.

GROG

Until as recently as 1970, every sailor in the British Navy got an issue of dilute rum. Prior to 1740, the issue had been neat and was the equivalent of one pint per man per day. Needless to say 90 per cent of the men were absolutely rat-legged for most of the time and

Admiral Vernon decided that enough was enough. He introduced the diultion of the ration in 1740, the new and unpopular measure being immediately christened 'grog' by the men, to whom Vernon had long been known as 'Old Grogram', that being the type of material that his highly distinctive boat-cloak was made out of. Naturally, the word 'groggy' is derived from the same point.

HAMBURGER

The first part of the word often causes confusion these days, but when the dish and the term first caught on in America, it was as a Hamburg steak. It was the Germans who introduced the idea to the States some time around the close of the 1880s, when the American idea of a good steak was to get a cow, pull the horns and tail off, and cook what was left. When they saw the emigrants messing up prime meat by mincing it up only to reform it into little cakes, they nicknamed the end result with the derisory Hamburg steak, which is a slur not unlike Bombay duck, Welsh Rabbit (and it is 'rabbit', not 'rarebit') or Glasgow capon.

HOT-DOG

This nickname for America's other great culinary contribution to healthy eating came into being as the result of a famous drawing by the Hearst cartoonist, T. A. Dorgan, published in 1903.

As soon as the Germans introduced frankfurter sausages to the New World, the Americans began to devour them voraciously. The particularly obnoxious-sounding 'wienie roasts' were being held in backyards across the entire continent from very early on in the twentieth century, but it was Harry M. Stevens, the man who held the food concession at New York City's Polo

Grounds, the home of the New York Giants, who first came up with the idea of selling these suspect items in a heated roll, with different relishes. Stevens instructed his vendors to go around selling them as 'Red-Hots' presumably because of the colour of the sausages. The idea really caught on and they sold like, well, hot-dogs! Dorgan, who was predominantly a sports cartoonist, encapsulated the new craze in a cartoon showing the sausage inside the roll as a dachshund, which was then a nationally recognised symbol of anything German but, unfortunately, this ended up doing more harm than good!

The American public, who love a good health/medical scare better than anything, with the possible exception of lying on the trick-cyclist's couch, was soon buzzing with rumours that their new staple diet contained dog - meat, or even dog itself. The Coney Island Chamber of Commerce banned the use of the term anywhere within their development, and ordered all signs to be erased and replaced by those advertising 'Coney Islands'. Anyway, the scare died a natural death and the now familiar 'hot-dog' crept back home to stay.

ICE CREAM SUNDAE

Evanston, Illinois, is not the only town in the American Midwest that lays claim to the origin of the term and the development of the multi-coloured abominations themselves, but it is the most often cited.

America has always been a nation where the Bible and ballistics go hand in hand and the bulk of the populace seem ever prone to and capable of a rather disturbing capacity and depth of religious devotion, or devotion to religion, which is probably more accurate and to the point. Many American states like Illinois, where it was considered quite all right to carry a gun on Sunday and shoot those who tried your patience just that little bit too far, but where the selling of ice cream sodas was thought to be a frivolity tantamount to blasphemy, passed legislation to prevent such sales on the Lord's Day. Now the problem with this was that, having left church, most of the sane members of the community were all too ready for a bit of sinful frivolity, and the soda-foundation owners were more than willing to oblige, so a side-step to the new laws had to be found. This was forthcoming at the opening of this century in the form of the ice cream sundae. Sickly sweet syrups, which had previously been used for flavouring the soda waters, were added directly to the ice cream and sold for the same price. The spelling of 'sundae' could well have arisen as a kind of 'get out of that' gesture to the outraged Bible-thumpers.

INTOXICATED
The expression 'name your poison' comes closer to the mark than most would suspect, for, in pure terms, an intoxicated person is one who has been shot to death with poisoned arrows.

The story starts off in Greece where *toxon* was their word for a bow. When they started producing distillations of vegetable matter to make toxins in which to dip their arrows, the word *toxicon* was applied. Since alcohol is itself a distillation, its effects were referred to as 'intoxication'. In current English, 'toxic' still means poisonous, and 'toxophily' the practice of archery.

JEANS
Almost every year, some fashion expert or another prophesies the end of the jeans era, but the public, blissfully unaffected by such prognoses, continue to pay outlandish prices for the privilege of wearing them. When the material was first introduced to this country,

it was as an import from Genoa and went by the name of 'jene fustian' because Gênes was the French name for that city. A later major manufacturing centre was Nîmes, which produced something called *serge de Nîmes*, that getting corrupted to the now familiar 'denim'.

KEEPING UP WITH THE JONESES

If there is one current expression that sums up the concept of fashion and whatever it is that constitutes style, it is this. If there is one way of keeping up with the Joneses, if not get a long way ahead of them, it is to roar round in, for example, a Ferrari, that name being nothing more than the Italian equivalent of 'Smith', words like 'ferreous' being directly linked. The main point of bringing this up is to illustrate that someone announcing that he trundles from traffic-jam to traffic-jam in a four and a half pint Smith, does not somehow conjure up the same image as does the man in the 2.5 litre Ferrari – and image is what the style game is all about.

Anyway, back to the expression. In 1913, a cartoon of this title began a long and successful run in the *New York Globe* and dealt with the problems that faced those who felt the need to maintain 'front'. The strip was penned by Arthur Momand and was originally planned as 'Keeping Up With The Smiths', but, as his then neighbours were actually called Smith, and the idea had evolved from some of the ritualistic manoeuvres that he went through with them, he decided against the title, but went for the next common name that came to mind.

KICK THE BUCKET

One of the favourite foods for fetes and the like used to be whole, roast pig. Whichever animal was lucky enough to be selected was unceremoniously strung up by the back legs from any convenient beam and bled to death. Failing to enter into the spirit of things, the pigs were never exactly overkeen on the procedure and kicked about a bit before giving up the ghost. Since the French for a beam used to be *buquet*, we ended up with 'kicking the bucket'.

KNICKERS
When Washington Irving (1783–1859) wanted to produce a comical work that dealt with the trials and tribulations of the first Dutch settlers of New York, or New Amsterdam as it was, he wrote it as if by the hand of the totally fictitious Diedrich Knickerbocker. Illustrated editions of the book, some by the hand of George Cruickshank, always portrayed the male characters in the traditional Dutch costume which included the billowy trousers that are gathered at the knee. 'Knickerbockers' soon became a jocular term for the kind of underpants worn by women and, when the garments themselves became more brief, so too did the name!

The ice cream dish that rejoices in the name of 'Knickerbocker Glory' was given its name because the gaudy colours of the ingredients were reminiscent of the silky trousers shown in the illustrations.

LUSH – A
As a term for someone who, whilst not yet a full-blown alcoholic, would do if you wanted one in a hurry, this has its origins in England but is far more commonly used in the States. Up until about the end of the last century there was an actor's club that called itself The City of Lushington and used the Harp Tavern in Russell Street, London, as its meeting place. Alcoholism and/or drugs always seem to have gone hand in hand with the

acting profession; perhaps it is the tedious affliction of most of that calling who feel the need to be larger than life in all things, that produces the need for a prop of one kind or another. Things were little different then either, and the marathon drinking sessions undertaken by the 'Lushes', during which they swilled down anything that didn't need chewing, were as infamous as they were legion.

MARZIPAN

The Arabic for a seated king is 'mauthaban'. What on earth, you are no doubt wondering, has this got to do with marzipan! Well, the Venetians issued a coin that was made of gold and depicted an enthroned Christ as its main design, so everybody started calling them 'mauthabans'. Long after the coin had passed from circulation, its specific weight remained as a measure for dry goods, but, by now, its name had altered to 'marzapane'. One of the few commodities sold by this peculiar weight was, you've guessed it, marzipan. The term entered English as 'marchpane' before modifying to something more like the Italian. So, if the old Venetians and the Arabs hadn't been the two greatest trading nations of their time, constantly rubbing shoulders with each other over deals, marzipan would have ended up being called Lord knows what!

MAYONNAISE

After the Duc de Richelieu had captured the port of Mahon in Minorca in 1756, he was feeling pretty peckish; all that siege and slaughter does tend to take it out of a chap. His personal chef, without whom he never ventured far, was given the job of knocking up a celebratory banquet with whatever he could lay his hands on, which wasn't much. But the man did the best he could and, in an attempt to brighten up some of the dishes, he concocted what is now called mayonnaise. The duke went a bundle on the stuff and promptly named it after his victory.

I know that this sounds about as false and phoney as a 'Dallas' star's smile, but it does seem to be the case. Apart from anything else, the spelling used to be 'Mahonaise', and it is far from being the only incident of its kind in history. After Napoleon had seen off the Austrians at the battle of Marengo, he told his chef to lay on something a bit special, the result being called 'chicken marengo' to this day.

NYLON
There have been hundreds of attempts to explain this most famous of all synthetic fibres name. The usual, and the least fanciful, is the tale that the word is made up from the initials of New York, and London, those being the two main point of patent registration of the manufacturing process. Even this is false, Du Pont themselves maintaining that there is absolutely no significance whatsoever in the name or the letters that go to make it up. None at all! Another thing revealed by that company is that 'Nylon' was not the only name put forward for consideration by the main board. One of the suggestions was 'Duparooh', that being an acronym of 'Du Pont pulls a rabbit out of a hat', but the more conservative members of the board soon put a stop to any trendy notions of that sort.

ON THE WAGGON
Many places, especially in the American West and Australia, used to have all their fresh water hauled in by waggon. By virtue of this fact, such places tended to be pretty godforsaken which meant that the people wanting

the water needed a very good reason to be there in the first place, and this reason was usually mining. Sitting around in the wilderness at night invariably produced a lot of drinking, those abstaining said to be 'on the waggon'.

PANTS

Medieval Italy saw quite a cult following of St Pantaleon and it produced a widespread craze for the name, so much so that there were thousands of little Pantaleons running around all over Italy, you couldn't move for them. Every culture experiences such fads in names; thanks to Charles and Diana we're in for an epidemic of Williams and Harrys. But this sort of thing has a nasty habit of backlashing in that the name becomes so common that intimations of stupidity start to creep in. In our own past, this has happened to Charles, which produced 'Charlie', and to Richard, which produced 'Dick' and 'Hick', that being an old variant of 'Rick', and this is exactly what happened to Pantaleon. Later, when early Italian pantomime was looking for a stock clown, the name was a foregone conclusion, especially since the name meant 'all lion' which sat so incongruously on the shoulders of the buffoon who was identified by his loose billowing trousers. 'Pantaleon' became 'pantaloon' which got cut down to 'pants', a term used here to describe undergarments but more properly in America to describe trousers in general.

PLUS FOURS

Now rarely seen outside comedy sketches, these oddities were designed for the golf course and derived their name from the fact that they fell four inches below the knee.

SANDWICH

John Montague, 4th Earl of Sandwich, was as well known for his devotion to gambling as he was for the rank corruption that pervaded every government office where he held a position. It is often said that he 'invented' the sandwich so that he didn't have to leave the card-table to waste time eating. This is so much rubbish; sandwiches were around ages before England had the misfortune to spawn Montague. They might not have been the elegant affairs presented to the Earl at the tables, but they were sandwiches nevertheless. It would not have taken a creature as inventive as man until the close of the eighteenth century to realise the benefits of folding meat or cheese in bread to make packed lunches or whatever. Montague did, however, give them a recognised name and respectability, something that they didn't have before he came along.

SUEDE

The very first items made of this type of undressed kid-skin that appeared in Europe were gloves imported by France from Sweden. Known as *gants de Suede*, they sold well which opened the door for other items which were simply called suede.

TANTALUS

The open-framed and lockable tantalus is well named from a character in ancient mythology who rubbed the gods up the wrong way so much that they came up with a special punishment, just for him. They consigned him to a cool lake in the middle of Tartarus, a hell set even deeper than Hades, where he was to be plagued by eternal thirst and hunger. If he stooped to drink, the waters receded, and if he reached out for the fruit that grew nearby, it too disappeared out of his reach.

Needless to say, the word 'tantalise' came from the same yarn.

TOAST – TO DRINK A

Wine-making processes have come a long way over the past few hundred years. That which used to pass for an amusing little wine would be an out and out joke now. Because of the excess sediment present in wines, pieces of toasted bread were put into the goblets to act as blotting paper for all the bits and pieces. With the considerable improvement of wine production methods the practice largely died out except when the guest of honour's health was being drunk – hence the current usage.

TOUCHING GLASSES BEFORE DRINKING

Now but a courtesy, this little habit has its roots deep in the soil of practicality and the days when dinner guests of people like the Borgias tended to say a few 'Hail Marys' before they risked any of the food or wine. Drinking yourself to death could be achieved with quite remarkable speed in such households. As a result, it became a common sight to see a host putting his guest at ease by volunteering to pour some of his own wine into the other man's goblet, he then returning the gesture. When poisoning became a bit old hat, a token touch of drinking vessels became a recognised sign of trust, even friendship.

TURNING THE TABLES

In, for example, William Shakespeare's day, the average run-of-the-mill table did not have its top fixed firmly in place; the reason for this being wholly practical in that it increased the item's versatility which was important since furniture was expensive then. A reversible top meant that one side could be used as a working surface without destroyed the polished dress side used for eating off. Should the dress side be uppermost when unwelcome guests came a-calling, a casual but pointed turning of the table-top was as broad a hint as the host could possibly drop that there wasn't a snowball's chance in hell of a bite to eat. The expression took on its current meaning due to the recipients of the gesture getting shown, or given, the rough side of things.

TUXEDO

The modern-day lady's man smoothing around in his tuxedo is nothing more than a wolf in wolf's clothing, because that's exactly what the name of his outfit means – wolf.

In 1814, Tuxedo Lake and the surrounding 13,000 acres of land in Orange County, New York State, passed into the hands of Pierre Lorillard in settlement of some debt. By 1886 the much-developed site was the hub of New York 'society' and all the big names had built houses there. After the Autumn Ball that was held on 10 October 1886, posing would never be quite the same there ever again. Griswold Lorillard, a direct descendant of the original owner, stunned the coagulation of co-eds and bright young things by turning up in what was basically the modern evening suit. He had picked it up on a previous trip to London where the fashion had been in vogue for quite some time, whereas tails were still the accepted norm in the States. Being far more practical, the dinner jacket soon caught on and took its name from the scene of its debut.

Long before the Whites turned up and began turning New York into the wonderland that it is today, the area was open country and very much wolf country, the Indians thus naming it *P'tuksit*, which literally translates as 'he who walks softly on round feet'.

TWEED
A fine material that got its name from a complete mix-up in 1826 when Locke of St James (they of 'bowler' shame!) received a consignment of 'tweel' from a Scottish manufacturer. The accompanying documentation looked as if it had been made out by a gorilla with a sprained wrist, and the clerk at the receiving house misread 'tweel' for 'tweed', no doubt making some subconscious connection with the River Tweed upon whose banks the material had in fact been made. Despite this sounding like a bit of a yarn the incident even gets a mention in the OED.

UPPER CRUST
This expression comes from the old practice of giving the best bits of whatever food was on the go to the more important people at the banqueting table. Loaves used to be simply ripped apart at the table and the tasty, crisp upper crust was always torn from the top of the loaf and passed to the head of the household and his cronies.

SPORTS AND PASTIMES

ABOVE BOARD

There's not a great deal to tell about this expression apart from the fact that it derives from the notion that a player should keep his cards in plain view at all times. In the 1600s, when this phrase was first used in print, 'bord' meant 'plank', 'bench', or 'table', this latter item being little more than a glorified bench in such times.

ACE IN THE HOLE

There are two main types of poker, five card stud and seven card draw, and the above expression derives from the dealing format of the latter. Every player gets two cards dealt face down to start with, followed by five more issued in rounds interspersed with betting. This issue of five are all dealt face up, the best combination dictating the betting. Even if someone appears to have a bad hand, this can be transmuted into a winning combination if the right cards, especially an ace, are in the 'hole', the two cards known only to the individual players.

ALSO-RAN

As a term for a low rater, this comes from the horse-racing world, specifically the racing commentators. Having given details of the placed animals, they usually go on to say – 'Also running were. . .'

AT SIXES AND SEVENS

This dates from a dice game that was popular in Chaucerian times, being something similar to the later game of hazard, which the Americans adopted and gave the ridiculous name of craps. It would be time-consuming and pointless to go into the intricate rules and finer points of these dice games (this means that the author hasn't got the foggiest about playing any of them); it is enough to say that, in the early version, the numbers six and seven created 'crossroads' in the play and, if all the players were playing such points, the game became so complicated that it was better to scrub all bets and start again. The number seven is still of prime importance in crap dice.

BACK TO SQUARE ONE

In the blissful days before the silver-screened cyclops began to dominate everybody's life, radio was the major home entertainment. The incunabula Beeb did its utmost to provide the best possible coverage of football matches and the like, and, towards this end, they arranged for papers to print a diagram of a football pitch divided into squares and placed on the same page as that showing the schedule of programmes. The commentators would feed the listener information as to which square the play was in and, after a goal, it was always 'Back to square one' because that was the kick-off point.

BADGER – TO

In days gone by, there was a particularly moronic 'sport' which was all the rage with the medieval red-necks. All that was required, apart from hordes of cider-swilling subnormal yokels, was a barrel to lay on its side to act as a retreat for the badger, and a few dogs. Every time the dogs succeeded in forcing the badger out of its barrel, the spectators would pull them off their unfortunate quarry which was returned to the tub again. The process was repeated until the badger was ripped to pieces. This intellectual pursuit of yore has left us with not only the expression meaning to harass another person, but also with a sad dearth of badgers.

BAZOOKA

Although this is now the almost internationally under-stood term for an anti-tank missile launcher, the word has not yet been granted recognition in military manuals.

During the Second World War an American radio comedian named Bob Burns was in his heyday. As a part of his act, Burns used a 'musical instrument' consisting of a bell-funnel stuck into a length of pipe. Since the GIs thought that the noise made by Burns with his bazooka (he called it that because of the 'Bazz-ooo' noise it tended to produce) and the noise made by the projectile leaving the launch tube were so similar, they transferred the name.

BLUE

In stark contrast to today, when sex is used to sell absolutely everything from underarm toiletries in plastic penoid containers to chocolate flake bars with thinly disguised intimations of fellatio that are about as subtle as a flying brick, the first half of this century saw some pretty diverse and carefully legislated censorship. No screen kiss could be other than 'straightforward' nor could it last longer than so many seconds, and, if it was necessary for a couple to be filmed in bed, both had to be fully pyjama-ed and nightied and have one foot firmly on the floor at the side of the bed, which is why actors in such settings were nearly always lying flat on their backs or sitting up in bed.

When it came to the risqué stage scenes that were popular in the burlesque days, the watch-dogs of public morals were no less vigilant. These stage-set, semi-nude portrayals of events, usually from Greek or Roman mythology, had to be absolutely static so that they could hide behind the slight relaxation in censorship intended for the 'artistic' picture post-cards that had come into such fashion in late Victorian times. Any movement on stage, no matter how slight and unintentional, invited heavy fine or closure of the theatre. Because of this, and in a half-hearted gesture to appease public dignity, tinted spotlights were used to light the scenes. It was soon established that blue was the colour best suited to the job for, whilst it allowed the overall image and impact of the scene, it tended to 'blur' the edges making the inevitable minor movements of the 'artistes' indiscernible from the body of the theatre. The same tactic was employed by places that put on the first strip shows, especially when the girls got into the more aesthetic parts of their acts.

BUFF

As applied to a devotee of any sport or hobby, this was a tag that was first used by the regular fire service of New York to take the mickey out of their irregular predecessors.

In the days before a formally trained and structured service, the city's fire-fighting had been undertaken by a loose body of volunteers whose heavy buffalo coats, which they wore for protection, became something of a badge of membership. Even after the professional service evolved, many of the 'buffs' would turn out to a fire, being more of a hindrance than a help according to the regulars. The firemen later spread the tag to embrace the people who simply liked to come along and watch some poor devil's house burning to the ground, and it is from this development that the word spread into general usage, having been used in on-the-spot television reports by fire department spokesmen describing the scene.

CLAPTRAP

This used to be two separate words and was theatre slang for a flashy gambit or ploy from the stage that was calculated to induce or force the audience to applaud. The thinking behind such tactics was usually quite sound; if you built enough claptraps into a cheap, shoddy act, the audience would sit there like a bunch of sycophantic seals clapping and barking their way through the entire sorry performance and end up thinking that it wasn't such a bad act after all. One of the best examples of a claptrap still in regular use, even on the television, is the one that never fails to appear in a magic act. When the chap on stage needs some piece of equipment or other, out staggers a scantily-clad blonde whose bombshell exploded several years ago, hands him his top hat with the rabbit hidden inside and then holds up her hands to the audience who applaud as if she has performed some earth-shattering feat. It never, ever fails!

CLIQUE

As far back as ancient Greece there were groups of people paid to attend theatrical performances, especially first nights, and clap, laugh, cry, etc. to help the play go with a bang. They didn't have a name then, but they did exist. In 1820, a certain Monsieur Anton Sauton opened up an agency in Paris to supply the ever-increasing demand for such people. The nickname 'Claqueurs' was a logical choice since *claque* holds a prime meaning of to clap or slap together. Not surprisingly they were not held in very high esteem by anyone, not even the people who hired them. The actors didn't want to have anything to do with them so the Claqueurs ended up forming their own little society of pariahs on the edge of the theatrical world. They eventually became known as 'Le Clique', not only because that means a drum and bugle band, but because it made a good ricochet term for 'claque'.

Everything progresses, so, just over a century later in the 1940s, teenagers were paid to turn up at the concerts of popular singers like Sinatra and scream at him, not in horror of course, but in feigned delirium and, unfortunately for some, this was the beginning of the end of what had been a very nice little earner. You see, the average pop-fan, not being the bovine incognitant that his manipulators had always assumed, only had to see this trick done a few times before he had got it off pat and was turning up at concerts screaming, fainting and generally chucking a wobbler all over the place for free. Perhaps there is method in their madness, for, as long as they can keep up a racket of their own, they don't have to listen to the one emanating from the stage.

CORNY

An Americanism for weak, hackneyed or over sentimental, this developed on Broadway to describe theatrical material that was in no way good enough for the city slickers and therefore had to go on tour in the sticks, where it was reckoned that the corn-fed audiences would swallow anything.

CRAP-DICE AND WHY WE CALL
THE FRENCH 'FROGS'

As already stated in the entry under AT SIXES AND SEVENS, only the Americans could come up with such a name for a dice-game! It is said that in 1803, a Creole by the name of Bernard Marigny introduced the game to New Orleans from France where it had been little more than a variant of hazard. Around that time, and indeed for many years beforehand, 'Jean Crapaud' – Johnny Toad – was a very common nickname for Frenchmen in general. It was certainly Marigny's nickname which is why the game of his introduction was first called 'Crap's dice'.

To understand why we call the French 'Frogs', how

Marigny and the dice game got their silly names, and why it is that France is internationally recognised by the fleur de lys, it is necessary to go back to the days when that which is now called France was part of the Frankish kingdom and was ruled by a man called Clovis.

In 493, or thereabouts, Clovis met, became enamoured of and married a comely wench who rejoiced in the unfortunate name of Clotilda. As soon as she had consolidated her position, Clotilda, who was a rabid Christian on the quiet, came out of the closet and embarked on a remorseless campaign to convert her pagan husband. Having been systematically beaten about the head with a Bible for seven years, the poor chap realised the hopelessness of his position and gave in. Yes! Jesus could have him for a sunbeam and, no doubt just to get a little peace and quiet for a change, he agreed to pop out and smite the Philistine in the shape of the Visigoths, a group of gentlemen who were less than chuffed at Clovis's conversion.

En route to the decisive battle, Clovis fancied he had a vision in which he saw his heraldic device transmute from its usual three golden toads on an azure background to three golden lilies. Presuming this to be a hot tip from head-office to indicate victory, he ordered such a banner to be made and, under it, he did chastise the Philistine sorely. Perhaps working on the assumption that anything's got to be better than having a trio of toads cavorting about one's banner, Clovis decided to retain the new design, later handing it down to that which became France.

It was Nostradamus, alluding to the old Frankish device, who, in the sixteenth century, coined the nickname 'Jean Crapaud'. About a century later, when the French court was permanently established at that greatest of all monuments to bad taste and vulgarity, Versailles, the courtiers drew the humorous division of toads and frogs between themselves and the ordinary

Parisians. Harping back to the glory of the Frankish kingdom, they considered themselves the toads and always referred to the city-dwellers as 'Les Grenouilles', frogs being generally the smaller and less significant of the two.

So, it was the French themselves who started calling themselves 'Frogs'; it did not arise as an insult levelled from outside the country due to the Frenchman's repugnant predilection for consuming the nether regions of frogs, as is often asserted.

FARCE

Scenery changes in medieval theatre could not be effected as speedily as is possible today. Because of this, short bawdy sketches called farces were put on to keep the audience amused whilst the sets were altered. They drew their name from the Latin *farcire* – to stuff – because they were literally 'stuffed' in between the main acts and generally padded out the entire performance. A bit like modern television where the adverts are more often than not better than the programmes that they 'interrupt', the farces were extremely popular and gradually grew into a theatre of their own, retaining their nickname.

In modern cookery, stuffing is still referred to as 'forcemeat', which is simply a corruption of 'farcemeat'.

FRISBEE

The whole craze started at Yale University where the students developed an irrational food-craving for the products of the Frisbee Pie Company of Bridgeport, Connecticut. The pies sold to the students on the campus came lodged in a stiff plastic plate which the students, subsequent to having devoured the contents of the sales package, employed in a manner other than for which it was intended. A quick-thinking local plastics manufacturing company noted the fad and produced moulded forms better suited to being flirted from one person to another than the pie plates.

HAM ACTOR
Very popular in the old black-face minstrel shows, where the 'acting' was very much OTT anyway, was a song entitled 'The Hamfat Man'. The song was a sympathetic dig at the second-raters who tended to drift into that very sort of show, and took its title from the fact that ham fat was then used to remove the heavy black make-up.

JAZZ AND BOOGIE-WOOGIE
Heavily influenced by the Hindustani 'jazba', which means something akin to violent desire, the word 'jass' was common black slang for sexual intercourse around the turn of this century in New Orleans. As a style of music, if one might call it such, jazz developed from the general type of music played in the brothels by resident bands who compensated for their lack of talent and polish with volume and enthusiasm. And that, as dey say, is jazz!

The second tag in the heading was directed to pretty much the same kind of music, but from outside the black community by the whites. Both 'boogie' and 'boogie-woogie', ultimately based on 'Old Bogey', a very old name for the devil, had already seen long service as synonyms for syphilis. The brothels and jazz-bars, which were nothing more than pick-up joints, did not enjoy a widespread reputation for paying great attention to hygiene, be it culinary or carnal, and it was generally reckoned that if you played around in such 'boogie-traps' you would pick up more than you bargained for.

JEOPARDY

An odd word to emerge from the world of pastimes and entertainment but that's where it comes from nevertheless. It came into being as the result of a game-call once common in many games in early France – *jeu parti*, which meant 'game divided'. It was the traditional announcement made in the closing stages of whatever was being played to indicate that only one point was required by either side to clinch the game. Both, therefore, were in jeopardy of losing!

JUKE BOX

At the risk of seeming to be afflicted with an obsession for the demi-monde of a bygone era, it is back to the New Orleans knocking-shops of yesteryear for the history of these unspeakable devices which, if periodically fed the appropriate emetic of fifty-pence pieces, will cheerfully oblige the simple-minded by regurgitating selections of their vile contents into the atmosphere *ad nauseam*. These turn-of-the-century instruments of modern torture, and their mid 1800s predecessors the juke-organs, which were little more than coin-operated, single-tune barrel organs, were quite properly kept firmly in their place, this being the bars frequented by prostitutes, and the then numerous brothels. Such joints were known as 'jukes', based on the Negro equivalent 'jook', which was ultimately derived from the Wolof African dialect word 'dzug', meaning a dissolute, dissipated and thoroughly debauched lifestyle. In other words, they are actually called brothel-boxes!

One of the unfortunate side-effects of the comparatively permissive attitudes of eras like the so-called Roaring Twenties, was that the bottom was knocked out of the brothel business. Many became simply bars, restaurants and even high-class hotels, and from these the canker of canned music and juke-boxes spread until, like today, there are even establishments where it is impossible to snatch a few moments of tranquil meditation astride the porcelain horse without having one's eardrums assaulted quadraphonically.

LEFT IN THE LURCH
This comes from the game of cribbage where it means to have failed to have scored thirty-one, or 'turned the corner' on the peg board used to keep the score, before your opponent has got 'home' and 'pegged out'. The term seems to be based on the French *lource*, which described an extremely unlucky or left-handed person.

LIMELIGHT – IN THE
In 1862, Thomas Drummond developed a new form of light that worked by burning lime. There were some limited experiments in lighthouses, but it was in the theatre that the invention really came into its own. The Drummond lamp produced a fairly accurate and direct-able beam that gave off very little heat in relation to its strength and intensity.

MAKING NO BONES ABOUT A MATTER
It was perhaps inevitable that, since early die were made out of bones, the nickname would stick to them after other materials were found to be just as good, not to mention cheaper. 'Makin' bones' was American black slang to describe the undignified cavortings and mum-blings enacted by some dice players before they throw the die. The experienced, and no doubt disillusioned, player simply picks the silly things up and throws them down the table, knowing that no amount of blowing, shaking in a particular way, or whatever, is going to make the slightest bit of difference to the outcome.

MUD IN YOUR EYE – HERE'S

A popular toast if ever there was one, this is the horse-powered equivalent of, for example, a modern racing-driver apologising to an adversary before the outset of a race about all the exhaust fumes that he is going to be breathing. You see, this was the customary, taunting toast before the beginning of a steeple chase during which everyone bar the leader got a healthy splattering of mud from the lead animals.

OFF THE TOP OF YOUR HEAD

This was born in the world of American television where the signal used by programme controllers to tell those in front of the camera to fill an anticipated gap by ad-libbing is a self-patting of the head, followed by the appropriate number of fingers held up to indicate the possible number of minutes.

OSCAR

For the first few years of the statue's life, it had no name at all. Then, in 1931, a young lady by the name of Mrs Margaret Herrick turned up for her first day's work at the Academy of Motion Pictures Arts and Sciences. One of the executives took her into his office to welcome her formally to the organisation and humorously introduced her to the statuette on his desk, informing her that she was then meeting the most important member of the Academy. Herrick made some comment to the effect that the statue looked just like her Uncle Oscar and, believe it or not, that was that. Having been searching for a name for some time, everyone in the Academy agreed that 'Oscar' projected just the right amount of dignity, yet retained that tinge of affection.

So, the statuette became Oscar and Herrick went on to become the executive secretary of the Academy. She later stated that her remark had not been a fatuous one; she really did have an Uncle Oscar to whom, in her opinion, the statue bore an uncanny resemblance.

PAINTING THE TOWN RED

After months on the trail, during which the only females that a cowboy saw all had four legs, a tail, horns and halitosis, your average trail-hand was not going to be content with a sarsaparilla and 'A Book at Bedtime' when he eventually hit town. Having got paid, it was straight over to the red-light section for a little light relief. He usually stayed there getting good and liquored-up before moving to phase two, which was shooting up the town. It must be remembered that the towns were not as large as might be imagined, so it didn't take all that many drunken cow-hands, accompanied by the lady of their choice, as often as not, to take red-light behaviour to sections of the community where it was far from welcome.

PASSING THE BUCK

In the poker games of the American West, a piece of heavy buckshot was used as a marker to indicate where the deal lay, or rather would lie, for as soon as a player picked up the deck to deal he passed the buckshot round a place. The overtones of an irksome responsibility exist because it was the dealer who had to put in the ante in most games. Back East, where things were slightly more sophisticated, poker chips were the norm, so a silver dollar was used instead of buckshot – hence 'buck' as a slang term for 'dollar'.

RAIN CHECK – TO TAKE A

Another Americanism that is steadily gaining ground in current English, this originated in the American ballparks, rainchecks being free passes issued to people who had bought tickets for a game that had subsequently been cancelled due to rain. When the game was rescheduled, the rainchecks were used for free admission.

SOUTHPAW

This rather peculiar term for a left-handed sportsman was coined in 1887 by the later famous Peter Dunne when he was but a cub reporter on the *Chicago News*. Working as a sports writer, he naturally had to cover the games of the then Chicago baseball team whose pitch ran east–west, as did the diamond-shaped home base plate where the batter received delivery from a westerly direction. Under these conditions, a left-handed batter would be facing south. Voilá, southpaw!

STEALING SOMEONE'S THUNDER

'Appius and Virginia' did not go down as one of the greatest successes in the dramatic career of John Dennis (1657–1734), the English playwright of dubious merit. This contribution to the cultural wealth of England did not last long after its opening night in 1709, and the only positive thing the critics found to say about the fiasco was that the device invented by Dennis to produce the thunder effects was far more realistic than anything else to date.

After the theatre had thrown out his play they put on a performance of 'Macbeth', having hung on to Dennis's thunder device to use in the first scene. When he heard about this, Dennis went along to a few performances and made a spectacle of himself during the play by shouting that the theatre company had stolen his thunder but wouldn't let his plays run.

WILD GOOSE CHASE

In the sixteenth and seventeenth centuries, bored young blades with no tenants to evict or wenches to molest would often organise wild goose chases just to pass the time. It was basically a mounted version of follow my leader, except that the lunatic leading the dance picked a route calculated to throw as many riders as possible. Since the whole exercise was but a dangerous and totally pointless waste of time as far as sane people were concerned, the name of this forerunner of the equally stupid game of chicken took on its current meaning. As for the name of the game itself, this was chosen from the flight-line of wild geese who were quite often seen strung out as were the participating riders.

CUSTOM, SUPERSTITION
AND TRADITION

ABRACADABRA

Although originally used in mystical chants and incantations, today this is more often used in scornful allusion to sham and hocus-pocus. The word would appear to be made up from the Hebrew *Ab* – the Father, *Ben* – the Son, and *Ruach Acadsch* – the Holy Spirit.

AMETHYST

This gemstone gets its name from a ridiculous belief shared by many of the ancients and given full backing by no less a bull-merchant than Pliny the Elder who, prior to popping his clogs in the year 79, recorded for posterity more inanities, half-truths and down right lies than have Hansard.

Apart from telling people things like how to temper their household knives with goat's blood if they wanted to chop up the odd diamond, Pliny also gave instructions on how to make amethyst drinking mugs that would prevent drunkenness, no matter how much the drinker drank. With drunkenness a major problem in Rome, the women went for this hook, line and sinker and they all rushed out to buy mugs made of this magical quartz, which got its name from the Greek *amethuskein* – not to intoxicate. Nothing changed, of course. Amethyst drinking mugs or no, most of the men were still getting blown out of their togas at every banquet, which is presumably why they demonstrated the good sense and foresight to start off in a fully recumbent position to reduce the risk of all those messy collisions with the marble flooring.

APRIL FOOL'S DAY

This all began in 1752 when we changed over to the Gregorian calendar in which the year starts on 1 January. In the previous Julian calendar, the New Year was celebrated with a festival that began on 25 March and ended on 1 April. To all intents and purposes, this was little different from our Christmas, right down to the exchange of gifts, gross self-indulgence and almost total lack of Christian spirit. After the changeover, 1 April remained as a sort of 'joke' New Year that was marked by token gifts and a bit of revelry before it became what it is today.

BACKING A HUNCH

In early England it was believed that touching the lump on the back of a deformed person could bring good fortune and protection from evil. This worked fine for everyone except the hunchbacks who couldn't go out without getting batted about the place by superstitious yokels. Gradually, the original expression of 'backing a hunchback' became 'backing a hunch' and took on a meaning of following one's intuition.

BED – GETTING OUT OF ON THE WRONG SIDE

This must be one of the best known superstitions which alludes to the person having got out of bed on the Devil's side. Folklore says that, all the time that you are asleep, the Devil and God sit at set sides of your bed fighting for your soul.

BEST MAN

In distant and wilder times, if your hopes of wedding the girl of your dreams had just been dashed by her father telling you that it was a case of 'over his dead body' and all that, you could always kidnap her! You rounded up some friends to help and from these you selected the best swordsman to guard your back as you made off with your heart's desire. He survives today as the best man and the rest of the gang are now referred to as the ushers.

BLACK CATS AND LUCK
Assuming that you are not a mouse, most consider it a lucky omen if a black cat crosses their path. Via the Roman invasion, we picked up this belief from the unlikely source of ancient Egypt where the goddess Bast was believed to assume such form to walk amongst her worshippers. Roman soldiers who saw service in Egypt adopted the belief and brought it with them to Albion.

BORN WITH A SILVER SPOON IN THE MOUTH
Although no longer fashionable, many upper-bracket babies got presented with a set of twelve Apostle spoons by their godparents. Now, a set of these was dear enough, but the inclusion of the master spoon was only within the reach of the very rich indeed, and it is this spoon that is the subject of the above expression.

BRING HOME THE BACON
In the year 1111, the Lady Juga decided that she had had just about enough of the local peasantry arguing and brawling with their other halves, so she set up the peculiar trust of the Dunmow Flitch. Her ill-fated aim was to encourage matrimonial bliss in and around the village of Dunmow in Essex by offering the little incentive of a flitch of bacon to any couple who could satisfy a panel of judges that throughout the year and a day prior to the claim there had not been a cross word between the pair. Unmoved, the local yokels seemed to prefer knocking seven bells out of each other, there being but eight successful claimants between 1244 and 1772.

CHRISTMAS CARDS

The whole beastly business was started off by a joker called Sir Henry Cole who, in 1843, decided that he simply couldn't be bothered to write the customary letter to everyone that he knew. He commissioned John Calcott Horsley to knock him up a suitably impressive design, got a few dozen or so run off, and sent them out embellished with a short personal message. The humble Christmas card was in trouble from the word go! Most who received them thought them an insult, the implication being that Cole didn't consider the recipients worthy of a full and handwritten letter. Later, in 1846, when Summerly's Home Treasury printed 1,000 of Cole's vile invention for sale at the price of one shilling, the Church waded into the fray criticising the design. Horsley's picture showed a few of the characters brandishing glasses of Christmas cheer, and the purists seemed to be firmly of the opinion that the only sort of spirit that should be around at Christmas was the Christian variety.

All of this was to no avail! The trend caught on, much to the delight of the printers and engravers – not to mention the Post Office!

CHRISTMAS STOCKINGS

The quaint and almost now extinct custom of hanging out stockings at Christmas originated from one of the yarns about St Nicolas that was brought back to England by returning Crusaders. The story goes that Nicolas heard of a poor man who couldn't afford a dowry for his three daughters so he was going to have to sell them off to the local flesh-factory. To save the timorous virgins from a fate worse than death, Nicolas crept into the house one night and popped sufficient gold to constitute a dowry into their stockings as they hung drying in front of the night fire.

CHRISTMAS TREES

This is very often stated to be a German custom introduced to England by Albert the Prince Consort, but this is far from the case. Actually, it is a British idea since it was St Boniface (680–754) who dreamt up the custom when he was over in Germany trying to convert the locals who, for their part, were heavily into tree worship. Realising that he was never going to break them of such habits, Boniface encouraged his flock to bring small trees into their dwellings at Christmas to symbolise the life-force of Christ.

The first Christmas tree of which there is any definite record in this country, was the one set up in 1800 by Charlotte, the German wife of George III. By 1822, it is known to have been introduced to Manchester by the presence of German merchants there, but it is fair to say that the custom was considered a bit non-U until Albert's 1848 tree was pictured on the front of the *Illustrated London News*, thus condemning the nation to picking pine needles out of its carpets for ever more.

CONFETTI

This is an Italian word that actually means sweets, specifically those thrown at weddings, as was once the custom. The confectionery had taken the place of cash, which ancient custom dictated but was out of the reach of most families. Later on, when even the wholesale throwing of sweets became too expensive for the peasantry, not to mention painful on occasions, an enterprising manufacturer started producing paper cut-out shapes of the traditional sweets and marketed them under the name of 'Confetti'.

DANCE ATTENDANCE – TO
It was once considered an absolute must for a bride to dance with every single man at her wedding celebration, and do so as many times as requested. Since this could often boil down to the poor girl being at the beck and call of half the drunken louts in the neighbourhood, 'dancing the attendance' as it was originally known, soon assumed its current meaning.

DEVIL TAKE THE HINDMOST – THE
Medieval tradition had it that Old Nick had a sort of school for scoundrels somewhere underground near Toledo. On 'graduation' day, all the successful students had to race down a long subterranean passage to get out, the slowest of them having to remain to serve a year as the Devil's imp, only to be released by the slowest student the next year.

GOOSEBERRY – TO PLAY
When spring had sprung and the countryside of Merrie England was teeming with courting couples, all of them had to have a watchful chaperon in tow. If they were lucky, their watch-dog might grant them a few moments alone by announcing that she was just going to pick a few gooseberries, which fall ready around April. At other times of the year, if a chaperon made such an announcement when everyone knew that there weren't any to be had, this was taken as unspoken permission for a few minutes hanky-panky before she returned empty-handed and coughing loudly, having been 'playing' at picking gooseberries.

Although today the expression is always applied to someone who is putting the dampers on the situation, in pure terms, it should apply to someone who sweetens the situation for a loving pair.

HAIR OF THE DOG

Quite why people persist in believing that alcohol will cure a hangover any more than a blow-torch will a burn, defies all reason, but there it is. A strongly held medieval belief had it that the only sure-fire cure for the effects of a bad dog bite was that the bitten man should avail himself of some hair from the offending animal and either eat it with some bread and milk, or make a poultice in similar manner and apply it to the bite. For the bitten man's sake, it is to be hoped that he had several friends willing to hold the beast down whilst he ripped a handful of fur from the cur, if not a vicious spiral would assert itself culminating with one very bitten man and one very bald dog.

HALCYON DAYS

We only use this expression in a metaphorical or meteorological way, but the Romans actually logged the Halcyon Days on their calendars as the fourteen days surrounding the Winter Solstice when the weather patterns do seem to be fairly tranquil. This lull they attributed to the kingfisher, a bird they considered to have the magical powers to calm the winds and the waves for the purpose of building their nests on the sea. The Greek for 'kingfisher' was *alkyon* and we got our spelling from the fancy that the name was derived from the Greek *hals* and *kuo* which mean 'sea' and 'conceiving' respectively.

HANDSHAKING

In earlier, not to mention more violent, days, men having good reason to distrust each other, such as heads of armies meeting for a pow-wow before the kick-off, would stand facing each other keeping hold of each other's right wrist with their right hands. The idea of this was to prevent either drawing sword, but the practice gradually reduced to a token grasp to indicate the lack of intent to draw arms. From this gesture of gross mistrust developed the custom so appropriately popular with politicians.

HEART ON YOUR SLEEVE – TO WEAR YOUR
The medieval equivalent of getting your latest maiden's name tattooed on your forearm was to turn up at the joust with her scarf or favour tied round your elbow. This method of publicly declaring emotions was considered a bit *infra dig* and took on a slightly pejorative aura that also carried overtones of insincerity.

HONEYMOON
It has often been cynically asserted that this term arises from the fact that the first month, or moon, of a marriage is all sweetness and light, but, when that period is past, the grimmer realities of holy deadlock tend to creep in. This may well be true, but it has nothing to do with the term, which derives instead from the Scandinavian and Germanic cultures where it was customary for newlyweds to drink a special mixture of herbs, honey and wine, this being thought necessary to sustain the couple through the protracted bouts of two-backed beasting and general carnal gymnastics that are prone to take place at such time.

Not that everybody found the brew to be wholly beneficial! Fully aware of the dangers of marrying a girl named Ildico who was less than half his age, Attila the Hun tarried long at his own wedding feast quaffing such terrifying quantities of the stuff that all were firmly of the opinion that their leader would be a widower by morning. Just the reverse happened! The greatest liberal ever produced by Germany staggered to his wedding bed only to gallop off into history for ever. The Scourge of Rome was dead; well and truly laid low by a slip of a girl.

HORSESHOES AND LUCK
There are quite a few things tied up altogether here, not least of which is the fact that a horseshoe on its side represents the letter 'C' as in Christ. Fire and iron were both once held to be sacred in some way, and these two elements came together in the manufacture of these items whose 'magic' was proved in the uneducated minds of our forefathers by the fact that they could be fitted almost red hot and nailed to a horse's hoof without the animal feeling any pain. Last but not least comes the legend that Satan once approached St Dunstan, who was renowned for his skill as a farrier, requesting to be re-shod. Pretending to fall for the trick, the saint tied Satan down and tortured him until he promised never again to enter a premises that had a horseshoe on display.

JUBILEE
In pure terms, this was a tradition of ancient Israel that only came round once every fifty years. Basically it was a time of national relaxation during which a jolly good time was had by one and all – even the slaves, because they were all set free. Most important of all was that the land was meant to rest as well, the law stating that it must lie fallow throughout the year – so who needed slaves anyway? No fools, these early Jews! Communication not being the all-pervasive mixed blessing that it is today, the beginning of festivities was proclaimed by heralds sent forth blowing their *yobels*, or trumpets made of rams' horns, 'jubilee' being a corruption thereof.

KETTLE OF FISH – A FINE OR PRETTY

'Kettle o' fish' used to be the Border's terminology for a fairly wild and uncivilised type of picnic centred round a freshly caught salmon cooked in a pot. Any cooking receptacle was once called a kettle, hence 'kettle-drums' which are shaped like cauldrons. Strong drink featured prominently at these affairs which usually degenerated into a beargarden with people being thrown into the river and the like. 'Pretty' used to mean cunning or tricky, and the expression was coined by the kind of people who wouldn't have been seen dead at a kettle o' fish, to describe chaotic events.

LICK INTO SHAPE

There is a charming medieval belief behind this phrase, which is based on the old notion that bear cubs were totally formless at birth and had to be quite literally licked into shape by their mothers.

MAUNDY THURSDAY AND MAUNDY MONEY

This, the Thursday before Good Friday, gets its name from the antiphon used in the ceremony. It begins *'Mandatum novum do vobis'* – 'A new commandment I give unto you' – this line being the signal for whoever was the star of the show to start washing the feet of a load of beggars rounded up for the occasion, in memory of Christ washing the feet of his disciples. From the fourth century onwards, this rite was expected to be performed by the Pope, all Catholic monarchs, priests and nobles. James II was the last British king to go through this ritual, all his successors preferring to give their more unfortunate subjects some money rather than come into such close personal contact with them.

It is often incorrectly maintained that the ceremony's name derives from the early English *maund*, which meant a basket, as was used to dish out bread and money to the poor. Actually, it comes from the early French word *mandé*, which meant a command or mandate.

MOTHERING SUNDAY AND MOTHER'S DAY
The former of these two days falls on the mid-Lent Sunday and, in pre-Reformation days came as a welcome break to all the fasting and self-denial that was so popular in the then Lent 'celebrations'. The customary thing to do was to visit the main, or mother church, of the parish bearing gifts and offerings. It was also a recognised day-off for one and all, those living away from home working in service and the like taking the opportunity to visit their parents as well, usually presenting their real mothers with small gifts. After the Reformation, the mother church thing faded away leaving only the domestic custom.

The second and far more widely observed festival is but the 'invention' of a Ms Anna Jarvis of Philadelphia. Never having heard of Mothering Sunday she came up with the idea in 1907, it being later formally recognised and adopted by Congress in 1914. Due mainly to the profit-motivated pressure exerted by the gift and greeting-card manufacturers, the custom soon swam the Atlantic.

NOT TO BE SNEEZED AT
In the seventeenth and eighteenth centuries, when the taking of snuff was deemed an elegant and gentlemanly thing to do, the practised sniffer was never expected to sneeze. Allowing yourself to do so was taken as a polite yet pointed indication of boredom, so, by extension, something that was not to be sneezed at was something worthy of note.

161

PANCAKE TOSSING

On the Shrove Tuesdays of yesteryear, one of the most popular pastimes used to be hounding prostitutes out of their quarters and tossing them violently in the streets in blankets to teach them the errors of their ways. When the authorities suppressed such quaint frolics, the population took to tossing their pancakes in races and the like, as a traditional reminder.

POLISHING APPLES

An apple is no more likely to be any dirtier than, shall we say, a pear, but people invariably rub apples absent-mindedly against their clothing before taking a bite. Although the Bible never stated the forbidden fruit to be an apple, most people incorrectly assume that it does, which produced the belief that to take a bite of an apple without rubbing the Devil's fingermarks from its skin, invited all sorts of ill-fortune.

RAINING CATS AND DOGS

Way back in history, cats and dogs were not only used as weather symbols, a dog representing the wind and a cat the rain, but people actually believed that certain of their behavioural patterns foretold of coming weather. If a cat chose to sit with its back to the fire, this meant that a storm was imminent. If it indulged in excessive face-washing, this heralded protracted wet spells. As for the dog, if it was seen eating grass and rolling on its back, this too signified heavy rain, and an inexplicable sudden retreat under a table meant a storm was due. Like all these things, there is no doubt some limited foundation to them, making them more or less as accurate as the forecasts that we get today.

ST SWITHIN'S DAY AND RAIN

Unfortunately for those who like to believe in such tales, 15 July is no longer anything like the same day as it used to be in the tenth century because of all the messing about with the calendar, and Swithin was never actually canonised. Anyway, on with the story! When he died in 862, the man expressed a wish that he be buried in the churchyard of Winchester Cathedral so that he could lie forever beneath God's heaven. Saints, just like pop stars, tend to gather more fans the longer they have been dead, and in 964 some well-intentioned monks decided that the old boy really ought to be moved inside to a more suitable resting place. You've guessed it! On the day they started work, 15 July as was, torrential rain delayed the transfer for a full forty days. Since another reason for Swithin having chosen his humble site was that he wanted the 'sweet rain of heaven to fall upon his grave', many associated with the project believed the rainstorm to be the irate saint passing comment on them from above.

Needless to say, it has never rained solidly for forty days and forty nights, from the middle of July right through until late August.

ST VALENTINE'S DAY

Neither of the two martyrs named Valentine had anything to do with the development of this festival, which has its roots much deeper in pagan times and the Roman feast of Lupercalia. This celebrated the rites of Februria, the Roman goddess of fertility after whom the month itself is named. As a sort of mating ceremony in which boys and girls were teamed up almost by lottery to go off and do whatever they fancied, this entered England with the Roman invasion and went down great guns with the locals. Ever anxious to seal off any avenue of pleasure, the early Church banned the more fun parts of the festival and replaced them with the exchange of gifts and tokens to symbolise spiritual union. To sever further any pagan connections, they also moved the day from 15 February back to the nearest saint's day, which just happened to be that of Valentine.

SKELETON AT THE FEAST

The ancient Egyptians had a gruesome little habit that could put you right off your meat and two veg. Before the beginning of a pig-in, they used to parade a skeleton around the banqueting hall before propping it up for all to feast their eyes on throughout the party. Before the guests were allowed to tuck in they were called upon to: 'Look on this! Eat, drink and be merry, for tomorrow you die.' The idea of this macabre practice was, of course, to remind all those present of the uncertainty of life and its fragile pleasures.

SNEEZING AND BEING BLESSED FOR IT

One of the bad things about the good old days was the Black Death, or indeed plague in general, which was an almost constant companion. As far back as ancient Rome it was common to hear a sneezing person being blessed because violent sneezing was strongly associated with the plague – hence the lines 'Atishoo! Atishoo! / We all fall down.' at the end of 'Ring A Ring O' Roses', which is generally accepted to commemorate, for want of a better word, the Great Plague of 1664.

SPILLING THE SALT

There have been innumerable attempts to tie this superstition to various events in ancient history, most notably to Judas at the Last Supper. However, it is far more likely that since the stuff was once so scarce and necessary to life, superstitions inevitably developed for no other reason than to make people damn careful with it. This did not always work out too well though! Some people got so scared that evil would be visited upon them if they did spill some salt, that instead of salvaging all the mineral accidentally dropped, they kept some back to toss over their left shoulder to blind the Devil whom they believed sat there waiting for a chance to catch them out.

THUMBS UP

Despite what the film industry would have us believe, there never were hordes of blood-crazed Romans waving a sea of downward pointing thumbs, thus indicating their desire to see a victorious gladiator finish off his fallen opponent. Quite the reverse, in fact! If that was what they wanted, the recognised gesture was in fact the now popular 'thumbs up', such gesture being made in an upward thrust to the heart; 'thumbs down' meant 'drop the sword and let him live'. Because bloody victory was the only true victory in the eyes of the bulk of the crowd, it was the gory 'thumbs up' that we inherited.

TOUCH WOOD

Virtually everyone in England must have said this and physically done so at one time or another. The expression, and indeed the custom, dates from the heyday of the Druids when trees were seen as the embodiment and dwelling place of all sorts of spirits. Should you wish to enlist the aid of any one of these deities, you had to go to the relevant type of tree and lay hands upon it whilst making your request.

WEDDING RING FINGER

Until the end of the sixteenth century, the wedding ring used to be worn on the right hand in this country. Around that time a belief sprang up that there was a special vein and nerve that ran from the third finger of the left hand directly to the heart. This was a strongly held belief, as indeed it would have to be in such times before anyone would have dreamt of associating anything so special with the left-hand side, which then had dark associations as many words in current usage testify. An ungainly person, especially a girl, is said to be 'gauche', that being the French for 'left'; 'gawky' is an old country term for a left-handed person, and 'sinister' is but the Latin for 'left'.